ENCOUNTER WITH WORLD RELIGIONS

ENCOUNTER
WITH
WORLD RELIGIONS

by

Robert D. Young

133914

ST. JOSEPH'S UNIVERSITY
BTQ416.Y6   STX
Encounter with world religions,

3 9353 00084 1187

THE WESTMINSTER PRESS
Philadelphia

COPYRIGHT © MCMLXX THE WESTMINSTER PRESS

All rights reserved—no part of this book may
be reproduced in any form without permission
in writing from the publisher, except by a re-
viewer who wishes to quote brief passages in
connection with a review in magazine or newspaper.

Scripture quotations from the Revised Standard
Version of the Bible are copyright, 1946 and
1952, by the Division of Christian Education of
the National Council of Churches, and are used
by permission.

STANDARD BOOK NO. 664–20876–2

LIBRARY OF CONGRESS CATALOG CARD NO. 75–86531

Published by The Westminster Press ®
Philadelphia, Pennsylvania

PRINTED IN THE UNITED STATES OF AMERICA

To
Bernard Phillips,
who inspired my research,
and to
my wife, Louisa,
who endured my inspiration

Contents

Part Two

PRACTICAL IMPLICATIONS

Preface

This book contains very little of the kind of information usually found in books on world religions, though it purports to be about that subject. The author has assumed that persons interested in world religions have done reading in other books that do give this missing factual material. The aim of this book is much more circumscribed. It is to give an answer to the questions: How are other world religions related to Christianity? Can the uniqueness of Christianity any longer be supported? Information from the vast literature on world religions must sometimes be kept in the background so as to focus on the dynamic interaction between the Christian faith and other faiths.

Some readers may object to the limited scope of Christian doctrine that is treated. There is reference to the Christian concept of revelation, the doctrine of the incarnation, the Christian view of God—but to little else in Christian doctrine. The question arises as to how one can speak about the relation of Christianity to other religions without using the full spectrum of Christian theology. There are several ways to answer this objection. First of all, this does not seem to be the day of comprehensive systems. Even Paul Tillich's elaborate theology, though completed but a few years ago, does not seem to be durable qua system. Someday we will enter another system-building era, but there is too much uncertainty at the moment to attempt anything more than a fragmented approach to Christian doctrine. However, just because there is no attempt to relate Christianity to other religions in a comprehensive way is no reason to avoid the attempt in a more limited way, particularly since the doctrines treated in this book are crucial ones. It is amazing how many modern Protestant theologians write as if their sphere of interest were isolated from the rest of the world. The world is now too small and the network of communication too elaborate for such provincial theologies to endure.

To many, this book will have a thesis mentality. There are many quotations, notes, technical words, designed more to satisfy an examining committee than the average reader. This is to be expected, since the book in a longer form, with many more notes, quotations, etc., was a Ph.D. thesis for Temple University. (The title of that thesis, for anyone who would like a more extensive treatment, is: "Towards a Theology of Openness in the Encounter of World Religions.") Although many things were changed or deleted, it was impossible to remove the bookish flavor of the original.

Since the author is a parish minister, with a full round of preaching, calling, and administration, it is doubtful if time will permit an adequate defense or elaboration of what is written here, however much that needs to be done. If others will take up the task, and improve upon this work, even if they reach totally different answers from those of this author, the purpose of the book will have been served. What must develop in the years to come is a growing body of literature that deals with the subject of what it means to be a Christian and that appreciates the contributions of the other great world religions.

My thanks are due to all my teachers, particularly the head of the Department of Religion at Temple University, Dr. Bernard Phillips, who is a guru of excellence. I would like to thank also the librarians and staff of the Philadelphia Divinity School who were most generous in allowing my use of their fine facilities. Many others have helped with the typing and proofreading, especially Mrs. Charles Cummings,

Mrs. Leonard Alton, Mrs. Robert Johnson, and Mrs. Barry Flewelling. There was also the patience of an understanding wife and family, and that of two fine congregations: Woodland Avenue Presbyterian Church of Philadelphia and Westminster Presbyterian Church of West Chester, Pennsylvania.

R.D.Y.

West Chester, Pennsylvania

Introduction

Many books on the theme of the encounter of world religions assume a homogeneous Christian faith, which meets the well-defined and homogeneous faith of another major religion: Hindu, Muslim, Buddhist, and so forth. However, this assumption is a large one, for every religion has infinite variety. It is Christianity in its variety that meets Hinduism, for instance, in its variety. The problem is further complicated by the fact that Christianity's variety is not just in major divisions—Protestant, Catholic, Greek Orthodox—nor in the further division of these into national churches, major denominations, societies of the clergy. Within each of these there are all points of view. A Baptist in the United States, for instance, can be Northern or Southern, ultraconservative or liberal, ecumenically-minded or isolationist, revivalist or social gospelist. To keep in mind the variety, while giving valid content to the genus word "Christianity," is a difficult task. Yet, difficult or not, in books dealing with the encounter of religions an attempt should be made to indicate what kind of faith within the variety is the participant in the encounter.

This book takes its start from a type of Christianity that has formed the background of the author's own outlook and that might be called "evangelical." Thus, it deals with a theology that is a recognizable participant in the variety of streams that flow into Christianity. In fact, while this stream has existed in most eras of Christian history,[1] it has been

15

without doubt the major one that has carried Christianity to other countries in the last one hundred and fifty years of missionary activity. Yet evangelical Christianity, by working with precise Bible-based creeds and a desire to convert men to the Christ, has usually lost its elasticity. This produces the irony that the type of Christianity least suited to meet other religions is the type that is most in evidence on all the frontiers where faith meets faith.

This evangelical position, which has produced such mission slogans as "Win the world for Christ," we have termed "theological exclusivism." In its unqualified form, it has thought the historic Jesus Christ to be the "only way," and has called on other religions to capitulate to this point of view. True and serious dialogue, with the possibility of finding truth in other religions, has been ruled out at the start by the exclusivist. It will be argued that this unqualified approach will no longer do. One can show that there is in the theological basis of exclusivism, particularly the theme that God was in Christ, far more flexibility than most evangelicals imagine. Furthermore, and contrary to Hendrik Kraemer and others, it is not necessary to have a narrow Christocentric theology to have a basis for the missionary movement.[2]

From whatever point of view, there is admittedly a dilemma that faces any theologian who wants to be both committed and yet open at the same time. This dilemma was well expressed in a recent article by Kenneth Cragg in which he asked the question: "Is the church in the world among the religions . . . either forfeiting truth to enable openness, or foregoing openness, and so making a criminal privacy of truth?"[3]

This dilemma can be resolved by giving up the conviction about Christianity's uniqueness, and taking the position of Symmachus. It was Symmachus who said of Christianity that such a great mystery must have more than one road to it. However, to depart from theology into some form of relativism is no advance. The paradox of Christianity's need to be universal as well as unique arose in theology. The most adequate answer, if any, must arise in theology too. The thesis we will pursue is that the only way to do justice to both a uniqueness that can breed intolerance and a universalism that can degenerate into relativism is by reconsidering some form of logos Christology. Such a reconsideration resolves the dilemma by deepening the commitment to the historic Christ until it becomes a commitment to all men in their religion. This solution sees Christ's incarnation and atonement as having significance for all men and not only for those who *consciously* acknowledge his Lordship. In place of the imperialism that often characterized the mission of the church, logos Christology gives a basis for the "boundless communication" that must characterize all the interaction between faiths in the coming years.

Most of the attacks upon exclusivism, with concomitant pleas for tolerance, have not been rooted in Christology at all. They have come from outside the theological field—from philosophy, psychology, history, comparative religion, and the like. However, exclusivism stands or falls upon the doctrine of revelation rather than upon an altruistic wish for a "faith for this one world" or upon facts presented by some other discipline. Outside disciplines may raise the question of tolerance—historians may show the bad effects of the Crusades, for example, and comparative psychologists may show how the Crusade mentality is present in the twentieth century—but only a wrestling with the Christian revelation itself can either give the Christian faith openness toward other faiths or close the door toward them.

In the past century or more, along with exclusivism has gone a missionary drive that has given a crusading appearance to the Christian faith. In what Kenneth Scott Latourette calls "The Century of Advance" a tremendous missionary effort was created, much of which rested on a theology that "there is no other name under heaven given among men by which we must be saved." For instance, in 1910, at the climax of the success of this movement, mission leaders met at Edinburgh to study mission motivation and practice. The theme of that conference was "The Immediate Conquest of the World." This militant attitude, the roots of which go back to the Pietist revival of the seventeenth century, has gone hand in hand with colonial expansion, the idea of progress, and the "white man's burden." What we are dealing with in the Christian faith is not an exclusivism that remains provincial and quiet, but one that is a hard-driving force. An exclusive religion that has a desire to "win the world in our generation" becomes an intolerant religion that can live neither at peace with other religions nor in fruitful interchange with them.

An example of the type of Christian exclusivism that has predominated in the mission field is found in Julius Richter's inaugural address before the senate of the theological faculty of Berlin on his appointment to the chair of the Science of Missions.[4] According to Richter, mission writings should be "the trumpet call of an advancing army." Other religions are to be studied so as to be "conquered." The climax of his theological exclusivism is contained in his summary:

Mission apologetics is that branch of theology which in opposition to the non-Christian religions, shows the Christian religion to be the Way, the Truth and the Life; which seeks to dispossess the non-Christian religions and to plant in their stead in the soil of heathen national life the evangelic faith and the Christian life. . . . It takes its position in the theological system as a new branch of apologetics which has still to be developed. In its method, it must be guided by the fundamental principle that its object is not so much to defend Christianity as to supplant heathenism.[5]

A position such as Richter's is not the only one that has motivated missions; a humanitarian passion stemming from the Enlightenment has also been at work. But the former is a dominant view, as any casual readers of the *International Review of Missions* may determine. It has been even more dominant since the Barthian influence through Hendrik Kraemer.

It is only natural that the first setting for the encounter of the Christian faith with non-Christian faiths should be in the mission field. And it is not surprising that the most militant statements of the Christian faith should be found in missionary literature. However, at the same time that a missionary apologetic was developing, the situation was complicated by the rise of a new science that in respect to methodology alone was a threat to the missionary motive. This was the science of comparative religion.

It is convenient to consider the development of comparative religion in two phases. The first might be dated roughly from Max Müller's *Chips from a German Workshop* in 1867 up to, but not including, Hendrik Kraemer's *The Christian Message in a Non-Christian World* in 1938. The chief characteristic of Müller's work was the unquenchable thirst for religious facts. The sacred books of the East were studied and translated; its civilizations were described, often with a Schopenhauerian fascination. The disciplines of prehistory, archaeology, ethnology, Sinology, Indian studies, Near Eastern studies, and so on, thrived, producing a mass of new data and methods. In referring to the thirteen-volume *Encyclopedia of Religion and Ethics* (1908–1921), with so many of its articles given over to the collecting of information, W. C. Smith observed: "I see it as typifying a culmination of the first great stage of scholarship in this field: the accumulation, organization and analysis of facts. This stage began, one may say, with the Age of Discovery, when Western Christendom reached out to the rest of the world, probing, exploring, gradually becoming aware of peoples and places far beyond its erstwhile horizon." [6]

There were several reasons why this stage was inimicable to Christian exclusivism. For one thing, the scholar deliberately took a stance outside all religions, as Van der Leeuw put it, "hovering over objects like a God." Information was

collected faster than it could be digested, or related to Christian theology, and the hasty implication was that there was
nothing particularly unique about the Christian revelation.
Parallels to it in both cult and doctrine could be found in
other religions too. Thus, the mere publishing of comparative
facts made the Christian revelation no longer sacrosanct.
Then, too, the world was shrinking, and firsthand encounters
with the saints of other religions were being made that put to
shame the mediocre discipleship of most Western Christians.
For instance, when Vivekenanda spoke in Chicago at the
World Parliament of Religions in 1893, everybody noted his
evident spiritual depth and many were quick to question the
need for Christian missions at all. One newspaper, in com-
menting on Vivekenanda's appearance, spoke for these people when it said: "After hearing him we feel how foolish it is
to send missionaries to this learned nation." Therefore, all
the while Dr. Richter was developing a mission apologetic
that would "conquer" other religions, the comparative study
of religion was providing material that threatened to under-
mine the missionary motive altogether.

This threat to Christian exclusivism from the "first great
stage" of comparative religion was in more than just the
amassing of facts. There were several other presuppositions,
which, if substantiated, would have weakened the Christian
doctrine of revelation. One was the search for the origins of
religion. The search implied a naturalistic basis for all religions, Christianity included. These origins were variously
placed. Max Müller attempted to show the origin of myth,
and consequently the origin of the names of God, in solar
epiphanies. W. Mannhardt (1831–1880) replaced this theory
by one which said that a "lower mythology," an agricultural
one, preceded the naturalistic mythologies studied by Müller.
Next, E. B. Tylor (1832–1917), in his book *Primitive Cultures*, made the case for animism as the genesis of religion.
R. R. Marett and K. T. Preuss stressed a preanimistic
force as the origin, which they called "mana." Andrew Lang

(1844–1912) and Fr. Schmidt (1868–1954) tried to show religious origins in a primordial monotheism. The list could be extended and refined, but the simple point was this: If all religions were expressions of a naturalistic source, one that could be isolated and described, the case for a supernatural Christian revelation was weakened. If Vedic stories or Buddhist ritual have a naturalistic explanation, why not Christian stories and ritual? There was no way to keep the one above critical analysis and not the other.

Finally, along with the desire to find the naturalistic origins of religious ideas went a theory of evolution that was in keeping with Darwin's hypothesis, German idealism, and the general feeling of progress at the turn of the century. This theory was not always felt to be a threat to Christianity. Many of the *Religionswissenschaft* scholars were committed Christians in regard to personal belief. By them, Christianity was presented as the highest development in man's quest for God, the synthesis of all preceding eras. The Hegelianism of Nicolai Hartmann or Rudolf Eucken would illustrate such a friendly approach to Christianity, as would the religious a priori of the early Ernst Troeltsch. Even where the evolutionary theory was not made explicit, the scholars often assumed the superiority of Christianity, just as they assumed the superiority of Western civilization. Max Müller, for instance, in his book *On Missions* (1874), has an unquestioning optimism concerning the progress of the Christian enterprise. Regarding Hinduism, he says: "I do not shrink from saying that their religion is dying or dead. And why? because it can not stand the light of day."

Yet, to find the justification for Christianity's superiority by referring to norms outside Christianity's revelation, while at the same time treating all religions as natural and historical, was hardly a benefit in the eyes of the theologian. To the exclusivist theologian particularly, men such as Müller, Frazer, Grubb, Lippert, Grant Allen, and a host of others were taking divine revelation and giving it a this-worldly interpretation. The words of William Temple at the Jerusalem Missionary Conference of 1928 are a good summary of the theologian's evaluation of the "first great stage" of scholarship: "The comparative study of religion has commonly been pursued by those who had little or no personal conviction of the uniqueness of the Christian revelation. Comparative religion started with the assumption that all religions are on a level." [7] As a result, a high barrier was erected between the new science of the history of religions[8] and missionary apologetics. Fortunately, there was a second stage in the study of comparative religion which lowered the barrier and allowed each discipline to develop a more helpful interchange. This was the stage of phenomenology.

Phenomenology, developed as an intricate philosophy by Edmund Husserl (1859–1938), began to be used as a method for comparative religion by an ever-widening group of scholars.[9] These included the pioneers—Geraldus Van der Leeuw (1890–1950), Max Scheler (1874–1928), and Joachim Wach (1898–1955)—plus writers of the present day: J. M. Kitagawa, M. Eliade, R. Pettazzoni, W. C. Smith, J. Danielou, and others.[10] Van der Leeuw's classic work, *Religion in Essence and Manifestation,* might well be cited as the beginning of the popularity of this new approach. The characteristic change from the first stage of the study of comparative religion was that phenomenology recognized itself as a descriptive science rather than a normative one. No longer did the scholar assume the role of judge-advocate. Instead, he was analyst-interpreter. This change has far-reaching implications, especially concerning the question of Christianity's uniqueness and the consequent attitudes of tolerance or intolerance. It was as if phenomenology were giving theology the right to determine its own attitudes and relationship toward other religions. We cannot go into any detail concerning this new method for studying world religions. Suffice it to say that phenomenology was no longer interested in origins, and thus it was no longer interested in the presupposition that all religion had a naturalistic beginning. Furthermore, in collecting religious facts, phenomenologists were more wary of the hidden metaphysical presuppositions that often existed, and tried to guard against them. The earlier scholars, by their philosophical presuppositions, had a way of rationalizing theological statements, or of fitting them into an evolutionary framework. As a result, these statements were not allowed to speak for themselves but were transformed unconsciously into illustrations of the scholar's philosophy. With phenomenology, on the other hand, the entire gamut of religion was still under investigation—cult, dogma, and ritual—but it was treated as a given, the origin of which was outside the limits of a scientific method. The new type of scholar in *Religionswissenschaft* simply grouped the facts that he had found into meaningful patterns, then asked what their meaning was in their own times and in ours. There was no judgment made as to the metaphysical truth claims which these facts indicated.

Having been given the exclusive rights by phenomenology to determine the relation that Christianity ought to have toward other religions, theology, where it has treated the question in recent years, has given an equivocal answer. Sometimes it has followed the exclusivist extreme with men such as Hendrik Kraemer. At other times it has moved the other way, toward the liberal theology of Paul Tillich. We will discuss these two extremes at some length, with a definite leaning toward Tillich and what might be called "theological openness." However, either answer, or any combination of answers, must attempt to be obedient to Christianity's revelation in Christ and not to the demands of comparative religion or some other related but descriptive field. For instance, let us assume that someone disagreed with the militancy of Christianity and believed that the twentieth century calls for a more tolerant stance. That person could stand off from Christianity and pick from it ethical statements or theological doctrines that would complement other faiths and fit the sense of fair play inherent in the American mind. This person would then have his own personal faith, but he would not convince the Christian community. Or he might attempt to stand within Christianity and take a dominant motif such as love and filter out all the barbed statements, such as that "there is no other name under heaven by which we must be saved." However, this is to dodge the important fact that Christology, at least since Nicaea, has made Christianity one of the world's great exclusivist religions. Our task in developing our thesis is not to ignore Jesus Christ, but to accept the total demands he places upon his followers. The question to be raised is whether this faith forces us to subdue other religions. Or does faith in Jesus Christ have a depth to it that includes the truth and faith commitment of all men in their religion? We believe the latter is a defensible position and must become central in Christianity's *Weltanschauung*.

Part One

TOWARD A THEOLOGY OF OPENNESS

I

A Critical Approach to Kraemer's Doctrine
of Revelation

In view of what we called the "first great stage" of *Religions-wissenschaft,* from Max Müller to Van der Leeuw, it is easy to understand the liberal attitude taken to theology and missions in the Laymen's Report of 1932.[1] According to this report, Western Christianity had shifted unconsciously from an exclusivist position. "There is little disposition to believe that sincere and aspiring seekers after God in other religions are to be damned. . . . It [Christianity] has become less concerned in any land to save men from eternal punishment than from the danger of losing the supreme good."[2] The reaction to this was the monumental work of Hendrik Kraemer in his book which was the study guide for the Madras meeting of the International Missionary Council in 1938, *The Christian Message in a Non-Christian World.*[3]

1. KRAEMER'S POSITION

Kraemer's book, which he feels has never been refuted, treated the non-Christian religions as part of the more general problem of the relation of the Christian faith to the world. Unlike the Laymen's Report, the position taken by Kraemer was a classic statement of exclusivist Christianity. There was no place in it for a division of revelation into "general" and "special," with the possibility of truth existing outside special revelation. Both adjectives were thrown aside and "revelation" was reserved for what Kraemer felt to be the Biblical meaning of the term. That Kraemer's name persists in almost every major book of the last twenty-five years about the encounter of world religions attests to the strength of his statement. He seems to be the antagonist of any twentieth-century man who feels that the various religions are various paths up the mountain. This is the way his argument develops:

Using such terms as "Biblical realism" and "radical discontinuity," Kraemer tries to set the Christian faith off from all empirical religions, including the Christian religion. Clement of Alexandria and all others who see Christianity as the fulfillment of man's universal quest for truth are placed to one side and condemned.[4] Karl Barth and those theologians who see the Biblical revelation as *sui generis* are approved and praised. Revelation is not an ethical system, not an evolution of ideals, not a cultural phenomenon or philosophy. It is the "no" to all man-made systems. When a man reads the Scripture, according to Kraemer, he is confronted by the God who acts. The Bible, though in many ways a human and historically conditioned document, consistently testifies to God's acts and plans in regard to the salvation of mankind and not to the importance of religious experience and philosophy. Such an approach to the Bible, which he takes as the generally accepted position of orthodox Christianity, is what he means by Biblical realism. Once Kraemer develops this position in Chapter 3 of *The Christian Message in a Non-Christian World*, he never deviates from it in any of his writings, nor qualifies it to any appreciable extent.

What is the content of the Biblical revelation? Here Kraemer faces a paradox. If the Bible is not a set of ideas, and if it does not propose any theology, how can one set down any series of propositions describing it? Kraemer recognized this problem and often protested against an intellectualization of revelation. Yet, since revelation is the presupposition on which the prophetic and apostolic witness of the Bible is built, he assumes that something can be said about it and proceeds without arguing the point. What he outlines is the familiar threefold pattern of God's activity, man's sin, God's grace. Karl Barth could have been the author of such an outline of revelation as easily as Kraemer.[5] Like Barth, Kraemer insists that it is the Word of God that creates the Christian apprehension of revelation. We speak because we have first been found by Jesus Christ. Faith is not man's corresponding organ which receives that which God has revealed. Not even here is there any continuity. John Baillie's statement that it takes two to have a revelation[6] is not discussed, but would certainly be rejected. In Kraemer's view the uniqueness of the Biblical revelation must be guaranteed, free from religious speculation.

While there is a "radical break" between God and man, it is the incarnation, the "decisive moment in world history," that reveals God as the holy and loving Travailer for the redemption and restoration of the world. Man, for his part, is fallen. He is caught in his rebellion, confusion, sin, and finiteness. Man has no principle whereby to judge whether a revelation has been given, nor to distinguish between special and general revelation. Kraemer is very critical of Tillich's formal principle of ultimate concern, which can be experienced outside the Christian faith. Also, he protests Tillich's belief, expressed in a discussion at the Bossey Ecumenical Institute, that there is a universal logos, a structure of reason, which is not affected by the Fall.[7] For Kraemer, all the points of contact between God and man are created by God. Man is totally in rebellion. Repentance is the only human element in the structure of the Christian faith.

Kraemer develops at much greater length what he finds the Christian faith to be on the basis of Biblical realism.[8] He is not denying that the contents of the Christian faith might be stated differently than he has done, but insists that the starting point must be the same—"*an open, honest, and courageous religious confrontation with and orientation upon the concrete realism of the Bible.*"[9]

In the light of such a close kinship to Barth, it is surprising that Kraemer is so critical of Barth in his later book, *Religion and the Christian Faith*. His main objection seems to be that Barth has found no way to say anything positive about the world religions. The dialectic is reduced to a ponderous "no." The gospel tone is missing. To some degree, this criticism of Kraemer's is justified. Furthermore, Kraemer wrote his later book, *Religion and the Christian Faith*, so that the "yes" to other religions might be spoken as forcefully as the "no." [10] Yet, for all this, one wonders if his criticisms of Barth do not apply to himself as well. In fact, as we shall see later, Barth's "tokens of revelation" and his anthropology (which is stated in *The Humanity of God*) make him more open than Kraemer to world religions, despite his blistering statement entitled "The Revelation of God as the Abolition of Religion." [11]

At the moment, however, our aim is to present Kraemer's analysis rather than to be critical. Given his view of revelation, what attitude is possible toward other religions? Kraemer would call his position dialectical and attempt to say many positive things about God's sovereign activity in the world at large, even while speaking his "no" to all human striving after God. For instance, the science of comparative religion is praised.[12] It has uncovered the "noble quest for truth and for the liberation and widening of the human mind." [13] More important, the science of religion has uncovered the flaws and the all-too-human element in Christianity. One of the important distinctions for Kraemer, as for most neo-orthodox theologians, is the distinction between the Christian revelation and the empirical Christian religion.[14] The latter, as a historical entity, has no cause for boasting. Contrariwise, in the world at large, "God shines through in a broken, troubled way: in reason, in nature and in history. Otherwise the urge for truth, beauty, goodness and holiness stirring in science, philosophy, art, religion is incomprehensible." [15] All of this is Kraemer's attempt to say something positive about God's activity in the world, apart from Biblical realism.

Yet, the "no" to religion is much more pronounced in both books. Despite Christianity's parallels with other religions—and Kraemer knows these as well as does any other scholar —man is a sinner. This corrupts everything that man produces, including his religion. As clearly as Barth says that religion is unbelief, Kraemer says: "The mystic, who triumphantly realizes his essential oneness with God, or the Divine . . . , who by his marvelous feats of moral self-restraint and spiritual self-discipline, offers a fascinating example of splendid humanity, commits in this sublime way the root sin of mankind, 'to be like God' (Gen. 3:5)." [16] If the mystic cannot qualify for any insight into reality, much less can the ordinary man. "Hence the universal religious consciousness of man has everywhere produced the most abhorrent and degrading filth that perverted human imagination and lust can beget." [17] "The cross and its *real meaning* . . . is antagonistic to all human religious aspirations and ends, for the tendency of all human striving is to possess or conquer God. . . ." [18]

The passages in which Kraemer says something positive about the world and world religions could be multiplied greatly. But the negative passages, in which man's striving is seen as a product of his sin, are always more numerous. This is true even in the second book, *Religion and the Christian Faith*, though the book was written to counteract the strong "no" of *The Christian Message in a Non-Christian World*. One illustration of the negative emphasis is Kraemer's exegesis of Paul's Areopagus speech (Acts 17:16–34). This is an important passage, for Kraemer uses it as a direct support for Biblical realism.[19] Yet his treatment of it leaves much to be desired and suggests a possible bias in Biblical realism in its treatment of this and other Biblical passages. For instance, in Paul's speech occur these words, as Kraemer translates them: "He [God] made from one every nation of men to live on the face of the earth, . . . that they should seek God in the hope that they might grope after him and find him." It is interesting to note that when Kraemer exegetes this sentence he gives full weight to the verb "grope" but no emphasis to the verb "find." That is, it seems as if he brings to the passage the idea that men before the Christian era search for a God they never find. The search is a form of *hubris,* and the verb "grope" is appropriate. However, to admit that the religious man, apart from the revelation in the historic Christ, could find God would weaken the whole structure of Biblical realism. Therefore, the verb "find" in this passage is overlooked. One suspects that there are many passages that are never allowed to speak freely because they have been forced into a preconceived mold. Not only so, but one suspects that there are many other passages that have been neglected—passages that give a broader interpretation of the people of God, and that suggest that many unknown people will come from the east and the west and sit down in the Kingdom.

Before criticizing Kraemer, however, we should mention two other of his concepts. One of these concerns the so-called "point of contact." The treatment of this topic is much fuller in the Tambaram Conference book, *The Christian Mission in a Non-Christian World,* and reflects the practical wisdom of the missionary statesman. Because man, even in his fallen condition, seeks after God, there is undeniably a point of contact for the message of the gospel. However, the usual meaning of the phrase "point of contact" has not related to the openness of man to God, but rather to the meanings of doctrine or cultic practice that are similar in two or more religions. This more common use of the term Kraemer rejects, and with good reason. When missionaries seek for such contacts, they always harbor the hidden conviction that a slightly better point of contact would make the preaching more successful, forgetting that it is Christ and the Holy

Spirit that are the agents of insight and change of life. A more important criticism according to Kraemer is that there is a tendency, when one looks for points of contact with various religions, to forget that religions are living wholes and not an odd assortment of specifics. For instance, the Chinese high god, Shangti, is referred to in various places in classical literature as having personal traits. It is easy to think that there is a similarity here to the personal God of the Christian religion, when actually Chinese culture cares very little for personality in the divine.[20] In any event, Kraemer concludes from such illustrations that the term "point of contact" has little use as a missionary or theological concept.

A second term that Kraemer would like to eliminate is that of "fulfillment." This concept is really closely related to the phrase "point of contact," but Kraemer treats it in a much harsher way. The reason is obvious. A "yes" can be spoken to the fact that God creates his own point of contact whereby the gospel can be communicated. That the term "fulfillment" can be used of Christianity's relation to the world is open to too much misinterpretation. Kraemer calls its use "self-defeating and self-contradictory." The word has too much connotation of continuity and evolution to be recoined. Its use prevents revelation from being seen as the radical self-disclosure of God in Jesus Christ.

2. A CRITIQUE OF KRAEMER'S EXCLUSIVISM

Much space has been given to Kraemer because of his impressive scholarship and his strong defense of a very dogmatic Christian position. He is the antagonist of all the earlier comparative religion scholars and of all later scholars such as Radhakrishnan, Toynbee, Hocking, Heiler, and others who plead for tolerance in today's world. When Visser 't Hooft writes on the mission of the church[21]—or Lesslie Newbigen,[22] or Edmund Perry,[23] or Heinrich Frick[24]—they follow pretty closely the line taken by Kraemer on revelation.

Furthermore, while nothing can be called a typical Christian position, certainly the missionary movement of the Protestant Church in the last hundred years has developed primarily with some form of exclusivism in mind, even where it was not articulated as Kraemer has done. Yet, is this position of Kraemer's satisfactory on his own grounds of Biblical realism? Let us attempt to list a few objections. In each case, the aim will be to criticize from within the stance of Christian theology, which is the only effective way to criticize exclusivism.

a. *Are all parts of the Bible accepted in Biblical realism?* Kraemer has a most commendable desire to allow his insights to be shaped by the Word of God. But just what does he mean by "Word of God"? If it is the Bible—and certainly this is the inference in the term "Biblical realism"—then there are certainly other facets of the revelation that are not touched on. For instance, W. E. Hocking points out that there is no significance given to hell in any of Kraemer's books.[25] What then is the risk in the world religions' not coming to terms with the Christian revelation? Apparently none at all. It is not that Hocking wishes to have Kraemer include a statement on the doctrine of hell, for he feels that Kraemer's common sense has filtered it out. The implication, however, is obvious. If one element in revelation can be ruled out, for whatever reason, then the other elements do not stand on exactly the same authoritative basis. The same conclusion can be drawn if the theologian says, "All the elements in the Bible are true, but only some do I care to emphasize." Any attempt to single out parts of the revelation introduces the human element, since the revelation does not divide itself. If there is a human element, however slight, then where is the much-talked-about "radical discontinuity"?

Barth, for all his dogmatism, seems on safer ground with his "Three Forms of the Word of God." [26] The word preached rests on the word that is written, and both are in a "trinitarian" relationship to the Word incarnate. It may not

always be clear how these three are related, but it frees Barth
from any wooden, literal interpretation of the Bible. Kraemer
might speak of the revelation in personal terms, as being
God's decisive event in Jesus Christ. But the term "Biblical
realism" focuses the revelation too exclusively on the Bible
itself and leaves him open to such criticism as Hocking's.

b. *Has the mystery of revelation been preserved?* There
are many statements in Kraemer about the mystery of revelation. One forceful statement puts it thus: "The mystery
of God's essence, as is demonstrated in all ages and all
religions, is to be concealed, to be hedged around by the
shuddering awe of inaccessibility; the mystery of the divine
Will, as lies in the nature of the case, has to be announced." [27] However, having laid the sources of the revelation in "the shuddering awe of inaccessibility," he proceeds
to outline the Christian faith and ethic in a way that is
quite accessible. From then on it is not the mystery that he
is witnessing to, but the theologian's statement of the mystery. Despite all Kraemer's protests to the contrary, the net
result of his Biblical realism is a set of propositions that are
set off from culture, philosophy, empirical Christianity, and
world religions.

Actually, a stress on a more undifferentiated mystery could
have at least two positive advantages that are consistent with
Kraemer's own aims. One would be to prevent the encroach-
ment of *Religionswissenschaft* into the unique domain of
Christianity. The science of religion, if it is true to its methodology, must stop at the edge of mystery, though not necessarily at the edge of the theological statement of that mystery. In the words of Van der Leeuw, "Before revelation,
phenomenology comes to a halt." Kraemer has not relied
on mystery as a point of defense. Rather, he has stated the
revelation with such clarity that the mystery is all but lost
in a series of affirmations, which must then be defended
against contrary affirmations.

Another advantage in allowing mystery to play a more

important part is that the consciousness of mystery produces humility. Kraemer has a great deal to say about humility, but it is always produced by the content of the revelation— God's activity which judges and redeems all men. Before this activity, all Christians have radical intrepidity and radical humility. They can be humble at the same time as they are saying that all religions are the man-made attempts to be as God! But while humility may be produced by a sense of sin and the reception of grace, so is it produced by "the shuddering awe of inaccessibility." The former are always mentioned by Kraemer as the basis for humility; the latter, seldom.

c. *Can the word "fulfillment," in all its meanings, be dispensed with, as Kraemer tries to do?* As we have already seen, Kraemer dislikes the word "fulfillment" as a term by which to characterize the relation of the revelation in Christ to the non-Christian religions. However, this term is ambiguous, and it is not at all evident that all its meanings are to be dismissed. For instance, Herbert H. Farmer, in an early criticism of Kraemer, pointed out that if the other religions are held to be a set of ideas and the Christian revelation is conceived as an act, then there is no fulfillment.[28] Aesthetic, or objective, truth (the I-It) is in another dimension entirely from the existential truth (the I-Thou). In this sense, Kraemer could be right in saying that the event of Christ does not fulfill the religious ideas of other religions. However, this use and refutation of the word "fulfillment" does not exhaust its meanings when applied to the Christian revelation. A further question is whether the Christian revelation fulfills the religious aspirations and longings of men of non-Christian faith. If the answer to this question is yes, then there must be some "preparation" outside the Christian revelation, and even truth.

Why is it that Kraemer is so reluctant to allow "fulfillment" to be used, in any sense whatever, of the relation between the non-Christian religions and the revelation in

Christ? Farmer believes that the reason lies in a theological axiom that precedes Kraemer's choice of Biblical data. This axiom is that the basic relationship in which God stands to man is one of absolute sovereign will. In accordance with this axiom, the principal relationship in which man confronts God is conceived to be a relationship of complete and unqualified submission and obedience. This is certainly a defensible theological position, and the exclusivism that results is understandable. However, the presupposition should be out in the open. On the other hand, and this is more important, God's relationship to man of fatherly love, which is also a defensible theological position, and which could rest on another set of verses than those which Kraemer uses, is scarcely treated at all. Farmer's conclusion is well worth pondering: "Sovereign will standing over against the will of man is not—I do not know how to put it—is not such a holding, binding, cleaving, seeking, yearning relationship as the love of a father which cannot and will not let men go; and I believe that as the mind is filled with the one thought or the other, so one's attitude is unconsciously determined in the matters under discussion, as in other things."

d. *Can Kraemer's dialectical approach do justice to other religions?* Usually when Kraemer uses the word "dialectical" in relation to the world religions, there is not the tension of paradox—the risk—that the word normally conveys in modern theology. Stephen Neill, who is a Barthian of sorts, notes this of Kraemer's books, particularly *Religion and the Christian Faith*. Neill feels that the "yes" and "no" are on parallel lines rather than in creative tension.[29] When Kraemer applies the dialectic, it is like seeing a western on television. The characters may vary, but the plot is essentially the same. While God's action in other religions is not localized, whatever appreciation there is of other religions is struck down by the "no" which is being said exclusively in the historic Jesus Christ. A dialectic without tension is not a true dialectic.

However, there is a unique sentence in Kraemer's writings which would be interesting to have explained. It occurs in his brief rebuttal to the critics after the Tambaram Conference. The context involves the possibility of a *theologia naturalis*. He says:

This rejection of a *theologia naturalis* as affording the basic religious truths on which the realm of the Christian revelation rises as the fitting superstructure, does not, however, *include* [italics his] denying that God has been working in the minds of men outside the sphere of the Christian revelation and that there have been, and may be now, acceptable men of faith who live under the sway of non-Christian religions, products, however, not of these non-Christian religions but of the mysterious working of God's Spirit. God forbid that we mortal men should be so irreverent as to dispose how and where the sovereign God of grace and love has to act. Yet, to represent the religions of the world as somehow, however imperfect and crude it may be, a schoolmaster to Christ, is . . . a misunderstanding of the Christian revelation.[30]

These words are said so deliberately that it is hard to believe they were just written carelessly. Yet, if they were taken seriously, it seems impossible that the system he proposes would have such a rigidity to it. For instance, the term "revelation" could not be tied so exclusively to the historic event in Jesus Christ.

It is interesting that Karl Barth, whose doctrine of revelation focuses on that which has taken place (and is still taking place) in Jesus Christ, has a few openings in his theology through which to see God's valid work outside the historic Jesus Christ. For instance, in an essay entitled "Revelation" he has a section on "Tokens of Revelation." [31] Revelation, he maintains, is once for all, and yet it occurs on earth in the continuity of the occurrences of created things, and that means in the occurrences of natural historical life. The manhood of Jesus Christ is the primary and absolute means of revelation. No one would believe in the eternal word of God unless this token were given. But this primary and absolute token of revelation is in some measure reflected and paralleled, and in this sense repeated in the sphere of created things. These other tokens are not revelation itself, but secondary and conditioned means of revelation.[32] Such tokens are the words and deeds of Jesus, the prophets and apostles, the Sacraments, and even the Christian experience and exhibition of faith. Could Buddha or the *Analects* or Upanishads be tokens for the Christian's apprehension? Barth does not say so, but what is to prevent one's extending the list?

In both the quotation of Kraemer used above, in which he will not deny that some members of the non-Christian religions might be acceptable to God, and in Barth's tokens of revelation, no real injury is done to the theologian's commitment to Jesus Christ. No doubt Kraemer's definition of revelation would have to be broadened, giving more attention to the logos idea. But even so, his basic jealousy for God's revelation in Christ is not endangered. Taking Kraemer's statement seriously, it means that we witness to our revelation with more of a sense of the bigness of God, who transcends our finite grasp of revelation. As Gerald Cooke has affirmed: "We need not deny that God has authentically disclosed himself in the non-Biblical world in order to confess existentially that God's revelation in Christ puts all other revelations or claims to revelation, under judgment. . . . We cannot preclude in advance that God has also authentically revealed himself to the religious consciousness of man outside Biblical history." [33] Rather than this lessening the glory of God, the reverse is true.

e. *Can the Christian religion and the Christian faith be separated?* It is essential to Kraemer's system that the Christian faith be separated from the Christian religion. Almost all theologians who wrestle with the problem of world religions and who do it from Kraemer's point of view make the same distinction. This has many advantages. By separating the ideal from the actual, the "ought" from the "is," the Christian theologian is prevented from having to defend so much in empirical Christendom that is obviously not right —the religious wars and intergroup hatreds that Radhakrishnan points out so effectively, the lethargy of the church when it comes to solving prejudice and economic problems, and so forth. It is comforting to say that all these shortcomings are not built into the original revelation, and that the Christian faith must be judged by its revelation and not by its expression.

However, if this distinction is only one between the ideal and the actual, it is a truism that is not terribly important. Then every empirical example that Kraemer draws upon to show that other religions are "monistic, naturalistic, relativistic and eudaemonistic" can be challenged. Members of other religions need only point out that the Christian theologian has not grasped what their religion is really saying. Some non-Christian apologists are quick to use this approach. Radhakrishnan, for instance, is particularly adept at giving Hinduism a Western flavor and then saying that this interpretation has been inherent in Hinduism all along. Following this line of argument, we would then have to admit that any judgment on other religions made by the Christian is exceedingly difficult, if not impossible. All that could be hoped for would be a comparison of empirical forms, as *Religionswissenschaft* makes, leaving the ideal above criticism in each of the religions.

Kraemer, however, is not simply arguing for the truism— that the actual is under the judgment of the ideal. He seems to argue that the Christian ideal is of a radically different sort than the ideal of other religions. He calls the ideal in other religions "original stimuli." [34] These stimuli, according to Kraemer, are a product of a human "religious consciousness," whereas the Christian revelation is outside the human realm entirely, originating as it does in the sovereignty of God. But the question that can be raised against Kraemer's reduction of all religions to a religious consciousness is, How do you know this? A. G. Hogg—whose writing has that fine combination of broad sympathy and deep Christian commitment—asks Kraemer what this "religious consciousness" is.[35] Psychologically, it can be analyzed abstractly as a human factor that has certain causal potencies. "But in concrete fact, is not the so-called universal religious consciousness just the universal manifesting of a human response (for the most part a deplorably crude, wayward and reluctant response) to God's continually active endeavor to reveal himself to man?" And if so, Hogg argues, is not every religion founded on what is, in some sense, revelation—on a more or less effectually penetrative, even if sometimes only microscopically penetrative, divine effort of self-disclosure? [36] Accepting this observation as valid, we would have to broaden the definition of revelation. When Kraemer writes of the Christian religion (the empirical religion) that "the revelation . . . has in the course of history engendered many ideas, concepts and experiences that are subject to the vicissitudes of ordinary human development; but they are never adequate or to be equated with the revelation from which they flow". [37]—we would have to agree. But, using the same word, "revelation," we would have to add: Neither are other expressions in other religions to be identified with their revelation.

There is another, more direct approach to the question, Can the Christian faith and the Christian religion be separated? Given the fact of our human predicament and history, how can we jump out of our human limitations to know what the Christian faith is apart from the church which witnesses to this faith? Kraemer's theology at this point is very deceptive. He says: "The possibility of achieving the most dynamic form of real tolerance is to be found in the purely apostolic attitude of being an obedient and joyful *witness,* and not a *possessor* of the truth that God has mercifully revealed. . . ." [38] That is true. But the hidden assump-

tion is that while we do not possess *the truth,* we know it
with sufficient clarity to witness to it. It still has the nature
of being well delineated, and raised above the level of everything else that is human. If this is so, then Kraemer is writing
as though Ernst Troeltsch had never lived. The formulation
of the Christian revelation under the heading of Biblical
realism is just as much a human enterprise as every other
attempt to write theology. Edmund Perry, who follows
Kraemer, is much more consistent when he denies that the
gospel and the church interpretation of that gospel can be
separated. For him, "Christianity . . . [is] so inevitably
derivative from the Gospel as to be intrinsic to the Gospel
itself." [39]

Kraemer at times recognizes the problem in separating
revelation from empirical statements about that revelation.
In his essay "Continuity or Discontinuity," he writes: "The
Christian revelation itself is my authoritative guide. . . .
*The only difficulty I encounter here—and this really is a
great one—is that I have only a partial and imperfect understanding of the Christian revelation,* and therefore, but a
defective grasp of its standards of evaluation and judgment.
. . . Only the guidance of the Holy Spirit can gradually
bring a deepening of insight, sensitivity and pureness of
judgment." [40] The only comment to be made on this is that
while admitting the human predicament, he writes as if he
had a much more certain understanding of what revelation
is in its essence. Much more to the point are the lines of
the poet:

> Life, like a dome of many-coloured glass,
> Stains the white radiance of Eternity.

II

A Constructive Approach
to the Doctrine of Revelation

It is relatively easy to criticize the efforts of a Christian theologian who is attempting to maintain the utter distinctiveness of God's revelation in Jesus Christ. It is much more difficult to maintain this distinctiveness as a matter of personal faith and yet interpret it so that revelation is open to truth outside the usual scope of Christian vision. What is maintained here is that the choice between, say, Hocking and Kraemer is not an either/or. Starting with Nathan Söderblom and William Temple, and moving forward in history to such men as Alan Richardson, John Baillie, H. Richard Niebuhr, or Lionel Thornton, we can develop a position on revelation that is decidedly in between. It is interesting that none of these names, with the exception of Nathan Söderblom, appears in any of the books Kraemer has written. This is somewhat surprising in the case of William Temple. Temple wrote the Foreword to the Tambaram Study book, and has written with great penetration on the subject of revelation.

Obviously, on such a vast subject as the doctrine of revelation, nothing of an exhaustive nature can be attempted. What is proposed, however, is to state some aspects of the modern problem that will allow the doctrine of revelation to be true to itself and yet include truth from other sources as well. In listing some of these aspects, we must bear in mind two general considerations. One is that up until recent times, the doctrine of revelation was not discussed in any but a traditional formulation. Canon Lilley's book, *Religion and Revelation* (1932), was one of the first to make explicit a revision of the traditional view.[1] This does not mean that changes of stance were not being fashioned before Lilley's work, but rather that not until recent years has the gradual shift become more clearly worked out. The other general consideration is that the doctrine of revelation is vital to the missionary program of the church, which will be the subject of the last chapter of this book. In a very useful symposium on the doctrine of revelation, John Baillie introduces a group of essays with the remark that "more and more the missionaries are concerned with the clarification of the content of their message—a clarification that has been forced on them particularly by the rapid eastward spread of our Western mechanistic and secularizing culture, as well as by the heightened self-consciousness of some of the Eastern religious cults."[2] In the years since Baillie wrote these words, the twin forces of secularity and non-Christian self-awareness have made his observation only the more accurate.

We have chosen four aspects of the modern understanding of the doctrine of revelation on which there is some general consensus. Taken together, they lead to a broadening of Kraemer's view, without destroying his concern for the uniqueness of the Christian faith.

1. The traditional doctrine of revelation has broken down.
2. Revelation is more than propositional truth.
3. Revelation involves fallible receivers.
4. Revelation is confessional.

Of the four, perhaps the last is the most important. As confessional theologians, we give up the impossible task of proving Christianity to be superior to other religions. Instead, we are free to engage in witness and dialogue without the encumbrance of an outworn apologetic. Actually, it is a confessional stance to which *Religionswissenschaft* has been pointing. Out of this approach came W. C. Smith's reminder that all conversations between world religions should be "we" talking to "you" about "us." Let us consider these four areas respectively.

1. The Traditional Doctrine of Revelation Has Broken Down

The traditional view of revelation, which has been supported by Catholics and Protestants, was formulated with clarity by Thomas Aquinas in the thirteenth century. The major division of the knowledge of God was between natural knowledge and revealed knowledge. An appropriate diagram would look like this:

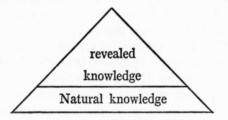

The "natural knowledge" of God was that knowledge which the human mind could attain without any kind of outside help. All the world religions, under this scheme, could have a kind of knowledge; but, however lofty, it would still not be of saving benefit. At best, so the medieval or Reformation theologian maintained, it was the knowledge that made man "without excuse" in the eyes of God (Rom. 1:20). But God did not leave man in this condition. In addition to the natural knowledge of God was revealed knowledge. It should be noted that the term "revelation" was denied to natural knowledge, since no supernatural aid was required. Revealed knowledge was the truth that was supernaturally communicated to men—the truth of the Trinity or of the incarnation, for instance. Several things about this kind of truth are important. In the main, it was thought of as propositional, and this fitted in well with the Western propensity for exact definition. Also, it was felt, particularly in scholastic periods, to be contained in the Scriptures, and therefore to be "possessed." The proof that a revelation had occurred was as external as the proposition itself, namely, miracle and fulfilled prophecy. Finally, the line between natural and revealed knowledge (shown in the diagram) merely separated two kinds of intellectual knowledge. Revealed knowledge was an act of God's grace to a man who was an *ens incompletum*, but nothing in the natural knowledge of man was to be contradicted by what God was freely adding on. This fact allowed Roman Catholic missionaries, particularly, to seek points of contact with other faiths, in the assurance that the path to saving knowledge was an unbroken one.

While the Reformation, the Enlightenment, and the Romantic era were not uneventful for the traditional view, the medieval position was not altered basically. As late as 1865, J. B. Mozeley, in his Bampton Lectures, was appealing to miracle and prophecy as the self-evidence that a revelation had taken place. Similarly, on the Roman Catholic side, the Vatican Council of 1869–1870 repeated the Tridentine phrase concerning the Bible, that it was written "at the dictation of the Holy Spirit." Revelation and the Biblical text were identified, and the traditional concept maintained, of man seeking intellectual truth and of God giving intellectual truth.

With the turn of the century, this traditional view of revelation began to break beyond repair. The effects of nineteenth-century theology, Biblical criticism, modern science, the comparative study of religion—all were playing their part in this break. As long as the diagram of the triangle was allowed to stand, it meant that the religions of the world were easily subsumed by Christian theologians beneath the apex of Christianity. These religions were denied the concept of revelation, and they were denied the salvation that was the accompaniment of revelation. Denied these, other religions hardly had the nature of religion at all. That Christians did take this attitude of superiority to other religions is easily documented. It was only by a theory of invincible ignorance that the salvation of men outside the Christian fold, which even human ideas of justice demanded, could be intellectually provided for. But such a position did not allow for dialogue between religions, since all the legitimate claims of the other participants were denied by the Christian before the conversation began. So it is fortunate that the division of natural knowledge from revealed knowledge broke down in a decisive way.

A very articulate statement of the breakdown was given in a Gifford Lecture in which William Temple took issue with this easy division of natural knowledge from revelation.[3] Still keeping to the terms in traditional use, Temple pointed out that the difference between the two was not the *content* of the beliefs examined, but the *method* of examination. Revealed religion accepted its beliefs by authority. As such, these beliefs lie beyond all natural theology. Natural theology, on the other hand, is "the criticism of actual religion and of actual religious beliefs, irrespective of their supposed origin and therefore independently of any supposed act or word of Divine Revelation, conducted with full understanding of what is criticized, yet with the complete relentlessness of scientific inquiry." [4] The distinction Temple made between natural and revealed knowledge *on the basis of method* has several important consequences. It keeps the Christian revelation from being an oasis of knowledge that is above criticism. As Temple said so forceably, "Let it then be frankly and fully recognized that there neither is nor can be, any element in human experience which may claim exemption from examination at the bar of reason." [5] That the Trinity and the incarnation are beyond the limits of the natural is a Christian claim that a scientific approach cannot refute. That there have been various types of belief in the Trinity—from the Cappadocian Fathers to Hegel—is a province in which reason must operate. Temple was aware that, by the traditional separation of natural and revealed knowledge, it had been easy since the *Critiques* of Kant to ignore revealed knowledge so as to concentrate on the religious experience of man. It is significant that Schleiermacher and Ritschl hardly use the word "revelation" at all. Others of the nineteenth century who were not doing theology were even less inclined to take the mysteries of the Christian faith seriously. The insulation from criticism, which Christian apologists had insisted upon traditionally, was working against its purpose, until nineteenth-century thinkers were more inclined to turn to natural theology for the right to believe in God. The newer approach, which Temple clarified, insisted that natural theology would have no real content apart from revealed theology, and that revealed theology—above criticism in its origins—must be open to criticism in its expression of those origins.

A final consequence of this methodological distinction is that the tip of the triangle, which had been reserved for the Christian mysteries, had now to be enlarged to include other religions too. If the Christian faith was above criticism in its origins, and only subject to criticism when these origins were expressed, then the same must be allowed for Islam, or Hinduism, or any other world religion. Temple recognized this. He said: "It is abundantly clear that a great deal, at least, of the actual religion of mankind is traced by its adherents to a supposed act of revelation or to a tradition so deeply rooted as to have the equivalent of divine authority." [6] This means that the tip of the triangle may open out like a lady's fan and include several revelations besides the Christian one. Each religion, to follow Temple's method, would contain truth that its adherents accept on authority but that is at the same time to stand open to the criticism of reason.

There is another way that Temple broke with the traditional division between natural and revealed knowledge. His argument rests on a prior demonstration, which we cannot pursue, that there is an Ultimate Reality in which the universe is grounded, and that this Reality is personal, with the ability to choose and to create. This being so, there is the consequent conviction that all things are in their measure an expression of a personal Will. The whole world is revelatory. In an oft-quoted statement, Temple summarizes: "We affirm, then, that unless all existence is a medium of Revelation, no particular Revelation is possible. . . . Only if God is revealed in the rising of the sun in the sky can He be revealed in the rising of the Son of Man from the dead; only if He is revealed in the history of the Syrians and Philistines can He be revealed in the history of Israel; . . . only if nothing is profane can anything be sacred." [7] This means that the distinction between revealed knowledge (God's gracious, suprarational gift) and natural knowledge (man's unaided quest for God) has given way to a distinction between particular revelations and general revelation.[8] Whatever the particular religion is that a man embraces, it will be a special revelation to him. All other religions than his own can be called general revelation. The base of the triangle—what has traditionally been called natural theology—is left with such fields as psychology, anthropology, sociology of religion, *Religionswissenschaft*. The world religions move above the line to the tip of the triangle, to the area of revealed knowledge.

So far, then, what Temple claimed is that the term "revelation" can be used validly of religions other than the Christian faith. This admission is a necessity for our modern day. It helps pry loose what we have called the exclusivism of the Christian faith. However, the Christian as theologian is in a peculiar position. He must say that valid revelations exist that have irreconcilable differences from his own. Temple's resting of the case for general revelation upon a personal Will who creates is far removed from the position of a Zen Buddhist, who places no importance upon deity, let alone divine personality or creativity. And yet the peculiar

position of the Christian theologian is that he is so committed to the revelation in Jesus Christ that he cannot allow
a status to general revelation that is independent of his
own outlook. His own outlook—the special revelation—can
hopefully be enlarged to give validity to other revelations.
But, by its very nature, special revelation cannot be *primus
inter pares,* else the stance of the theologian is exchanged for
that of philosopher or historian of religion.

2. REVELATION IS MORE THAN PROPOSITIONAL TRUTH

Nearly all modern writers, including Barth and Kraemer,
share the view that revelation is more than propositional
truth. Kittel's *Theological Dictionary of the New Testament*
states this as follows:

In the Old Testament, revelation is *not* the communication of
suprarational knowledge and *not* the stimulation of numinous
feelings. The revelation can indeed give rise to knowledge and is
necessarily accompanied by numinous feelings; yet it does not itself consist in these things, but is quite essentially the action of
Yahweh, an unveiling of his essential hiddenness, His offering of
Himself in fellowship.

The same thought is acknowledged about the New Testament:

Revelation is likewise understood, not in the sense of a communication of suprarational knowledge, but in the sense of a self-
disclosure of God.[9]

Seen from the standpoint of the Christian faith, revelation
is a divine self-disclosure, not just a fact disclosure. As John
Baillie puts it so well, "The modern teaching is not *from*
Subject to subject, but *of* Subject to subject." [10] God's activity in Jesus Christ ends in communion, not in academic
excellence. All the thought opened up by Martin Buber's
distinction between I-It and I-Thou is relevant here. I-It
applies to the identification of revelation with propositions.
I-Thou, the fuller and yet mysterious confrontation, applies

to revelation as communion between God and man through Christ, a communion in which God's will and purpose are discerned.

This firm twentieth-century position, in itself, is a help toward overcoming exclusivism, in that interpersonal relationships (man with man, God with man) have a mystery about them that is not present concerning propositions. Propositions can be possessed and mastered. They are static. The human mind, which sees propositional truth as bounded by clear-cut lines of demarcation, is always superior to that which it delineates. By the same token, when Christian faith is clearly packaged by the theologian and set in the midst of other world religions, which are similarly delineated by him, it is no wonder that he can feel fortified in mind and superior in attitude. But communion, though relying on propositions, is never fully described by propositions. Communion, even on the human level, has a mystery about it. Where the one person in the communion is God, it is questionable whether any language can be adequate, including categories that relate to personality itself. It is with this inadequacy of language in mind that the Christian theologian, who must of necessity use words to describe the event of God in Christ, should not have superior airs in confronting world religions. Built into his own understanding of revelation is the possibility that the overflow of what he has found might touch and intermingle with the mystery of other religions.

That revelation and mystery are related is a common observation of modern theologians. For instance, a few might be mentioned. Paul Tillich uses mystery as one of his marks of revelation. He points out the very penetrating truth that whatever is essentially mysterious cannot lose its mysteriousness even when it is revealed. It is not as if now that God has acted in Christ there is nothing further to be grasped.

Something more is known of the mystery after it has become manifest in revelation. First, its reality has become a matter of experience. Second, our relation to it has become a matter of experience. Both of these are cognitive elements. But revelation does not dissolve the mystery into knowledge.[11]

John Baillie, in his discussion of revelation, gives a similar statement. He says of the apostle Paul's use of the word "mystery": "The mystery becomes a mystery only in being disclosed, while at the same time, if it were fully disclosed, it would cease to be a mystery." [12] Father Bulgakoff, the Eastern Orthodox theologian, reiterates the same when he writes: "Mystery ceases to be a mystery if it is not disclosed; or on the other hand, if it is resolved or exhausted by the process of revelation. God is a self-disclosing Mystery." [13] All these scholars would affirm the importance of God's disclosure in Jesus Christ, and they would all affirm the finality of that revelation for themselves. Yet, in these days of the increase in knowledge of world religions, the mystery of revelation needs to be emphasized so that it can broaden and deepen the certainties to which we witness. Too many times the mystery of the faith is spoken of in a theological work but the general tone is not conditioned by the awe of the mystery. The mystery must so get hold of a theologian's viewpoint that, so far as revelation is concerned, he conveys the feeling that at best "we see through a glass, darkly."

3. Revelation Involves Fallible Receivers

One of the characteristics of the traditional view of revelation was its aura of certainty, which was permitted to no other human experience. Yet it is doubtful if the word "revelation" has any real meaning until it has been received by fallible men. A way of expressing this is to say that it takes two to make a revelation.[14] Furthermore, the coincidence of infallible God with fallible men is not infallible revelation. What is needed, suggests one theologian, is the word "to revelate," which could combine the human and the divine.

However, it has been hard to admit the fallible element in

connection with revelation.[15] Particularly is this noticeable in the way some theologians have approached the Bible and have attempted to hold its inerrancy while recognizing its discrepancies. From the days of Clement and Origen, one method of reconciling differences has been the reliance on allegory. Another has been to retreat behind the several senses any one passage might have. For instance, Thomas Aquinas quoted with approval the words of Augustine: Observe two rules, he said.

The first is to hold the truth of scripture without wavering; the second is that since Holy Scripture can be explained in a multiplicity of senses, one should adhere to a particular explanation only in such measure as to be ready to abandon it, if it be proved with certainty to be false.[16]

But, this is a difficult position. If I must believe what is the truth of Scripture, but have no way of knowing what that truth is, what has happened to religious certainty? Revelation must be indubitably true, and also unmistakable, or it fails to fulfill the function that medieval writers assigned to it. Of course, Augustine's and Thomas' hermeneutics were undergirded by an infallible church and an infallible spokesman of that church. This was a more consistent position than the Protestant one. But, it would not explain why their hermeneutical principle, which would destroy the certainty of revelation if applied by laymen, would not also destroy the certainty of revelation when applied by the church. Perhaps another doctrine was needed, namely, the doctrine of the Holy Spirit. But, again, the history of the church is the history of persons who were guided often in entirely conflicting ways by, as they said, the Holy Spirit.

The modern theologian, of course, has had to wrestle with far more than Augustine or Thomas. At least under the traditional view of revelation, the words of Scripture themselves were the *ipsissima verba* of God. The meaning might shift, but that which was to be interpreted did not. Under modern

Biblical criticism, that which was to be interpreted, the words themselves, was also apt to shift. A movement had taken place similar to that in astronomy, when Newton's theory that motion is over against a static background was discredited. The background—in this case the words of Scripture—was now in motion too, with the consequent threat to religious certainty. Yet the quest to preserve the Bible's infallibility persists in this modern day.

The strong appeal of Barth and his school is just at this point, that they can try to combine modern criticism with the older realization of certainty. Barth made no attempt to minimize the human element; in fact, he seems to use it to guarantee that a false reliance is not placed on the *ipsissima verba*. But this recognition does not seem to qualify his dogmatism. In the Bible, he says repeatedly, God speaks to us, and that is the Bible's authority. For Barth, to attempt to separate the human element from the divine in advance is an utter impossibility. It is enough that, paradoxically, that which is human can be the means of allowing the incarnate Word to speak to us directly. There are ever so many advantages in Barth's position, apart from satisfying the craving for certainty. He allowed the believer to be a modern man so far as accepting Biblical criticism is concerned. Furthermore, Barth has a strong appreciation for the church, as the unity in which and through which *Deus dixit*. This is obvious in his "Three Forms of the Word of God," [17] where Scripture and incarnate Word are related to the church's proclamation. There is no place for individualism here. Yet despite these commendable features, the implication of the human and fallible element is entirely ignored. It may be that Pascal is correct in saying, "We could not seek Him unless He had already found us." Yet in this aphorism there is a disguising of the fact that man counts for something. If grace is not a sheer miracle, then there must be some incipient faith awaiting the divine disclosure.

As E. L. Wenger puts it so succinctly: "Revelation is certainly God's act—it is not revelation otherwise—but when theologians say that revelation is divine activity and say no more, as if the copula expressed an identity, they are simply abusing language." [18]

One other modern attempt to avoid the fallible element in revelation is worthy of comment. This is Austin Farrer's discourse in the Bampton Lectures of 1948, *The Glass of Vision*.[19] Reading Farrer, with his delicate and graceful wit, after reading Barth, with his ponderous phrasing, is like watching a ballerina after a heavyweight fight. Farrer gives as his aim: "We believe that in the New Testament we can, as it were, overhear men doing supernatural thinking of a privileged order, with pens in their hands. I wish to make a fresh examination of this phenomenon." [20] He is not at all concerned with the subject of general revelation—and in this he resembles Barth. "I speak of the Christian revelation as Revelation par excellence. . . . The degree in which other faiths have something of revelation in them, and the manner in which they are related to Christ's revelation are matters which I well know to be worthy of discussion, but I beg leave not to discuss them." [21]

According to Farrer, there are three elements that should be considered in revelation—the historical events of Christ's life, the images that convey the meaning of that life, and the theology or philosophy that is the analysis and criticism of the revealed images. As the Bible does not contain "a line of theology and of philosophy not so much as an echo," this intellectual discipline is not discussed. His defense of event and image, however, is vigorous; and together they constitute revelation. Let us follow his argument:

Rather reluctantly, he accepts the modern criticism of the Bible's inerrancy. "We now recognize that the propositions on the scriptural page express the response of human witnesses to divine events; not a miraculous divine dictation." [22] In place of this, he begins with Jesus Christ as the primary revelation. However, this primary revelation, the event, is not complete in itself apart from its verbal interpretation by both Jesus Christ himself and the early church. The event is like a seed, and the interpretation is the necessary growth. But, and this is central to his argument, the interpretation is not inerrant propositions, but rather pregnant images.

Farrer does not attempt to limit the number of these images. He lists the dominant ones as the Kingdom of God, Son of Man, Israel as the family of God, and "the infinitely complex and fertile image of sacrifice and communion, of expiation and covenant." [23]

These tremendous images, and others like them, are not the whole of Christ's teaching, but they set forth the supernatural mystery which is the heart of the teaching. Without them, the teaching would not be supernatural revelation, but instruction in piety and morals. . . . The great images interpreted the events of Christ's ministry, death and resurrection, and the events interpreted the images; *the interplay* of the two is revelation.[24]

This is enough of Farrer's argument to make a few relevant observations. It appears that Farrer hopes to guarantee to images the plenary inspiration that scholars denied to propositions. However, this is difficult to do. Granted that the imagination and intellect are two modes of religious apprehension, the same criticism that applies to the one applies to the other. In Paul's writings, images and propositions are intricately mixed. It would be hard to say that propositional apprehension contained a human element and therefore an element of possible error, while images were given directly by God and contained no such element. Therefore, while Farrer's attempt to preserve the importance of the Bible along traditional lines is commendable, and while the poetical truth value of images does not have all the prickles of Biblical literalism, his attempt falls short before the same criticism that felled the traditional view of revelation.

There is a further observation. The mere listing of images without any criterion as to which ones are vital and which are secondary is open to all kinds of abuse. Some formal criterion, such as Tillich's ultimate concern, is needed. Wenger observes, and rightly so, that the concept of justification by faith is an image that certainly expresses, as no other category, an essential truth in the relations between God and man. It presupposes the thought of God as absolute sovereign and man as helpless criminal. But, to take this category as the chief image, as Barth and Kraemer have done, gives a lopsided picture.[25] What of the family images of Father and son, or the medical images of healer and sick? Farrer has no way of distinguishing these. Yet failure to do so can have great consequences in guiding the Christian church in its encounter with world religions.

There is one final issue relating to human fallibility that needs to be expressly stated even though it has been firmly implied throughout. It should be axiomatic that if there is any fallibility in revelation, as indeed there must be, that fallibility will be persistent, affecting a man before as well as after accepting the Christian faith as his own. Alan Richardson, for instance, claims too much in one of his illustrations. He refers to the blind man in the New Testament who first saw men "as trees, walking," and then was able to see clearly. Richardson's comment is: "The 'natural man' sees men as trees walking, and this seeing is itself possible only through the operation of God in general revelation; before he sees all things clearly he must encounter the touch of God's Messiah. . . . Thus, special revelation is not a concrete illustration of general revelation, but a correction and transvaluation of it." [26] Now, with much of this we would agree. There is a real sense in which the Christian commitment makes "all things new." But to compare the

Christian as a man who sees, to a non-Christian who sees
distorted truth, is to forget that human fallibility operates
after the Christian commitment as well as before it. Our
fellowship with the living God through Jesus Christ is the
krisis of everything we can say about that relationship, as
well as the *krisis* of non-Christian revelations.

The persistence of human fallibility among the committed
was effectively argued by Walter Horton, though from a
different point of view. Horton's burden is not that man's
sin or his finitude makes the vision of God imperfect at best.
Rather, he contends that revelation is nonsense unless it
derives its specific content from the world at large. Since
this content is continually growing, revelation must reflect
this growth too. Something of Tillich's "method of correla-
tion" is intended. "The meaning [of revelation] appears in
its true significance only when revelation is used to interpret and cast light on other truth. To rely on revelation
apart from other truth is as bad as to rely upon prayer without action. . . . The man who knows only Christ does not
even know Christ." [27] This thought of Horton's is a needed
corrective to that type of theological statement which implies that what happens in the Christian experience is enough
to cancel both man's fallibility and corruption, so that the
Christian man can speak as the voice of God and no longer
as a limited creature. The only thing that can be added to
Horton is a widening of his statements to include the religions of the world. Horton is thinking throughout his essay
of Western science and culture, and is contending against
any view that would tie revelation to a *sacrificium intellectus,*
thus violating "that reverence for all truth which liberal
Protestantism has—let us hope—made permanently a part
of the Christian conscience." However, there is no reason
to limit the word "truth" to the West. It may be that the
man who knows only Christ, and not the other religions of
the world, does not even know Christ! At least our fallibility
should make us open to this possibility.

4. Revelation Is Confessional

The heart of any attack upon exclusivism certainly lies in the realization that special revelation is confessional. This makes the adjective "special" synonymous with "historically conditioned" rather than synonymous with "superior." Briefly stated, the matter is as follows: "[Christian theology] cannot think about God save as historic, communal beings and save as believers. It must ask what revelation means for Christians, rather than what it ought to mean for all men, everywhere and at all times." [28] Something of what this means can be seen by comparing the early church with the early apologists of the church. In the New Testament community, there was no argument for the existence of God or the universality of the Christian faith. And, certainly, there was no argument concerning a common human conscience, unhistorical and supersocial in character. Instead, there was a simple recital of the great events connected with the historical appearance of Jesus Christ, and a confession of what had happened to the community of disciples. There was evident the tension of witnessing to something that could not be put adequately in words and that was bigger than argument. The "proof" of the Christian faith was what had happened in the church's historical existence by the historical event of Jesus Christ. Out of a visceral encounter—not merely a mental one—the early Christians could not but speak the things they had seen and heard. Now, this first-century witness—a community confessing its existence with God—is the only possible stance. Particularly is this so in the light of the work of Ernst Troeltsch and the *Religionsgeschichteschule*. The same influence that we noted earlier, which makes theology compatible with the history of religion, is what drives the Christian away from an academic claim for the superiority of his faith and toward the stance of a confessor. A clear statement of this stance is given in the writings of H. Richard Niebuhr, who puts his position as somewhere between Ernst Troeltsch and Karl Barth.[29] Let us follow the development of his position.

The crux of the issue is whether or not anything can be said about revelation that escapes the flux of history. Troeltsch had made it impossible to believe that this escape could be made. Before Troeltsch, liberal Protestant theology had given up the idea that it could know God apart from the human experience of God. This, in itself, was confessing a limitation on revelation. Theology, in the nineteenth-century thought of Schleiermacher and his followers, was empirical theology. God was not an object in himself, but only in human experience. This is not to underplay the significance of Schleiermacher, for empirical theology under his direction worked under human limitations with an effectiveness greater, if anything, than it had possessed before. But, the change that Troeltsch indicated, and that seemed to threaten the nineteenth century with an impossible relativism, was to show that our human nature (the basis of empirical theology) was a historically conditioned human nature. Nothing escaped this conditioning. Phrases such as "the natural rights of men," "the law of supply and demand," "the law of wages," were neither intuitions of pure reason nor deductions from absolute premises, but rather inductions from historical and social experience. Even Kant's unshakable "starry sky and moral law" is a product of Judaic-Christian tradition. In other words, we are historically conditioned thinkers who cannot describe the universal save from a relative point of view.

The sting of this relativism is even sharper when it is realized that the object of our consideration—Kant, for instance, or any historical person or system—is not the only thing that is time-conditioned. So are we, the subjects. Every observation of Kant is as much conditioned by our concrete existence as was Kant's philosophy when he wrote. Both subject and object are on movable platforms. This is why historians speak of history's having to be rewritten in each succeeding generation. There are no facts that stand still in a once-for-all fashion.

What is to be concluded then? Skepticism? Subjectivism? Not at all. Rather, there must be a critical historical theology that allows for four things when it speaks of revelation:

Coherence. No one can prescribe what form religious life must take in all places and all times beyond the limits of his own history. But he can seek within that history some intelligible pattern:

It [critical historical theology] can undertake to analyze the reason which is in that history and to assist those who participate in this historical life to disregard in their thinking and practice all that is secondary and not in conformity with the central ideas and patterns of the historical movement. . . . It may try to develop a method applicable not to all religions, but to the particular faith to which its historical point of view is relevant. Such a theology for the Christian Church *cannot, it is evident, be an offensive or defensive enterprise which undertakes to prove the superiority of Christian faith to all other faiths;* but it can be a confessional theology which carries on the work of self-knowledge in the church.[30]

Certainty. This is affirming that what is historically conditioned need not be untrue. Nor need the truth be clouded over with the subjective statement, "This is truth for me." It must be truth for me, else I would not be concerned to witness to it. But, it may be truth for my neighbor or for every man. Or, it may not be. The personal witness of certainty is in another realm from the purely academic claim that one religion is superior to others.

Faith. Since relativity touches both poles of the Christian faith, both the New Testament historical events and the history in which I live, and since relativity cannot account for the certainty to which Christians have confessed in every generation, it is an act of faith whereby we accept the reality of what we see in psychologically and historically conditioned experience. "If we are confined by our situation to the knowledge of God which is possible to those who live in Christian history, we are not thereby confined to a knowledge of Christian history but in faith can think with Christianity about God and in Christianity have experience of the being who is the beginning and the end of this historical faith." [31]

Verification. Revelation is not a form of solipsism, just because it is historically conditioned. Every confession of the Ultimate is subject to the test of experience on the part of companions who look from the same standpoint and in the same direction, as well as to the test of consistency with the principles and concepts that have grown out of past experience with the same community.

This, of course, is no well-worked-out theory of revelation. It is simply to point out an aspect of the doctrine that keeps the Christian faith open to other religions and rests its religious certainty on some other platform than an a priori judgment. Let us list some advantages of a confessional approach that are particularly relevant to world religions.

a. *The confessional approach to revelation limits the apologetic value of history.* One of the great souls in the Christian church, as well as in the field of world religions, was Nathan Söderblom. In what we have termed the "first great stage" of *Religionswissenschaft,* it was Söderblom who stood as a bridge between the scholars who appeared to threaten the Christian mission, and the Christian church. Writing in 1903, at a time when such men as Friedrich Delitzsch, the noted Assyriologist, had shown so many similarities between Babylonian and Biblical religion, Söderblom pioneered with using the term "general revelation." Many scholars feel that his constant reference to " '*Heilig,*' *das erste Wort der Religion*" ("holy," the first religious word) was the seminal thought for Rudolf Otto's *Das Heilige.* Rather than seeing comparative religion as a threat, Söderblom insisted that it is high time in this age of world missions that the church acquaint itself with the thought of the general revelation of God.[32] Yet, for all his understanding, Söderblom seemed to misuse history to prove Christianity's superiority.

Söderblom had a great awareness of the historical flux of revelation which, in confessional theology, must be combined with certainty. Of prophetical religions, he writes: "We cannot discover any gap in the historical and psychological continuity of the life of the prophet. . . . Neither can we in the prophetic religion draw a line around certain words or certain events and say here is God and revelation—there is man and nature. Even in the perfect revelation of God in the person of Christ, the divine and human are commingled." [33] Yet the confusion in Söderblom's approach is that he wanted to use history, and an analysis of world religions, to prove the superiority of historical Christianity. It is as if, from a historian of religion's point of view, he is comparing several movables (i.e., historical religions) and trying to arrive at a judgment that is above all flux.

Yet, this statement of Söderblom's intent is not quite accurate either. He used the idea of Christianity's superiority in a very ambiguous way. Sometimes he intended it to mean a full development within its kind, much as an oak tree would be the completion of a seedling. Thus he wanted to distinguish Christianity as the summation, or climax, of all religion from Christianity as the full completion of its own special revelation of God. The former he refuted; the latter he affirmed. Yet, alongside this he had a contradictory position. In expressing it, he wrote: "The Special revelation in which this revealed religion [Christianity] stands to the general development of culture is matched by the inner character which it possesses, which, *in comparison with any corresponding religions, marks it as superior,* not only in degree but essentially differing from them in those qualities which are common to all religions." [34] The qualities he used for comparison are those of the unity of God, his personality, involvement in history, etc.

Now, the simple fact is that neither use of the idea of superiority can be argued from the historical standpoint—neither that Christianity is fully developed as a particular kind of religion nor that it is best among the religions. There is no criterion of judgment that is outside the historical continuum whereby history can be judged in any absolute fashion. The Christian may witness to the finality of Jesus Christ and live so that that witness is incarnate. But, witness to the felt certainty of God in history is not the same as demonstrable proof. More sound is Söderblom's remark in an episcopal letter, "Conviction about God must build on an overwhelming personal experience of reality, not on an accumulation of facts accessible to all." [35]

b. *The confessional approach to revelation makes creedal formulations important but provisional.* A very useful analysis of various approaches to creedal formulation is given by Robert Lawson Slater. Technically his book, *World Religions and World Community,*[36] is outside the theological circle. Slater writes as a historian of religion. He has a great respect for the world religions in their particular concrete reality, and he defends no philosophical axiom that says that all the religions are saying the same thing—"united at the top," to use Hocking's phrase. He is content with showing that each religion can be historically unique without producing a threat to world community.

The importance of Slater for our present discussion is his demonstration that in each religion there exist three different attitudes to the truth which they see, though each religion seems to have one of these three predominate. Some are essentially nonconfessional. Hinduism is of this sort, as witnessed by the fact that modern Hindu writers are always protesting the sharp creedal differences they find in Western Christendom. Slater does make the point, though, that the objection is not so much to doctrine, nor to one doctrine's being more important than another. Rather, the Hindu has placed primary importance upon the vision of the Real behind all true teaching, and not upon the "way" to that vision. Usually, the uncritical Westerner becomes enamored with what seems to be Hinduism's indiscriminate tolerance, while having no passion to be led "from the unreal to the real, from darkness to light, from death to immortality."

At the other extreme from nonconfessional religion is the type of confession that Slater calls "subscriptionist." This is the type that the author feels predominates in the West, and is that which Eastern authors have in mind when they speak of "Western thought." The marks of subscriptionism are as follows: (1) a summary statement of the faith professed by the religious community; (2) a valuation of this statement as sufficiently precise and true; (3) a demand for subscription to the statement thus valued as the condition of membership in the community.[37]

It is this type of confessionalism, patterned after the traditional view of revelation, that makes the church intolerant and prevents world community. Slater observes that in the beginning of the church there was a general confession—a proclamation—"Jesus is Lord." Confess this, writes Paul, and "you will be saved." And it was this missionary hope of the new community that "every tongue" would confess this "to the glory of God the Father." But, this did not imply a sharp definition. Rather, it stimulated richness of thought and flexibility of interpretation. Subscriptionism came later with the movement toward consolidation and with the preciseness that Hellenistic thought afforded. The result, says Slater, is a tension even today within Christianity between a zeal for definition and a hesitation to press definition too far.

The third position, and that which the author prefers, is confessionalism proper. It is this which has similarities with the position developed by Niebuhr. Confessionalism is not afraid of presenting its revelation in propositions. In fact, a relativism that would dissolve all historic formulations of the faith would be worse than dogmatism. But, in whatever form the faith is cast, there should be a provisional attitude toward the formulation. Slater feels that Buddhism is a good illustration of this use of the word "confessionalism," in that the symbol of the Buddha character unites both Theravada and Mahayana Buddhism. He feels also that the Episcopal Church, among Protestants, has a strong confessional position. But, the key of confessionalism is a loyalty to one's faith expressed in broad creedal statements, and a tolerant respect for others.

c. *The confessional approach to revelation is optimistic.* Let us examine a statement of Richard Niebuhr:

Such a theology [confessional theology] is objectively relativistic, proceeding with confidence in the independent reality of what is seen, though recognizing that its assertions about that reality are meaningful only to those who look upon it from the same standpoint.[38]

This position seems to place a great limitation upon the Christian faith, as if it is forever confined within its segment of history. It is as if all the religions are as perceptive and yet as isolated as Leibniz' monads, reflecting the cosmos from their own point of view, but never really changing basic orientations. But the conclusion is not that we must accept the limitations of history and realize that we cannot get out of our time shell, as it were. Just as the primary revelation in Jesus Christ has been reshaped in every succeeding generation, so it will be in whatever world culture is emerging. This is not to predict a single religion for one world, nor is it to promote either radical displacement or reconception. It is merely to suggest that the histories that have shaped the primary revelations of each world religion are not a series of isolated streams. The historical context in which future generations will view Jesus Christ is a context in which the several streams of history have merged.

III

Revelation

and the Logos

There have been many scholars in ancient and modern times who have made use of the logos as a means of saying at one and the same time that Jesus Christ is Lord and Savior, and also that the Christ cannot be confined to one segment of history that began in Bethlehem. Thus, Justin Martyr called Christ the Word of whom all mankind have a share. According to Justin, all who lived according to reason (*kata logon*) are Christians—men like Socrates and Hera-clitus, as well as Old Testament saints.[1] William Temple carried the same thought into the modern day when he wrote: "All that is noble in the non-Christian's systems of thought is the work of Christ upon them and within them."[2] He maintained that Isaiah and Plato, as well as Zoroaster, Buddha, and Confucius, conceived and uttered such truths as they declared by the Word (logos) of God. Many Roman Catholic scholars of modern times could be quoted in exactly the same vein. The question arises whether such a broad interpretation of the incarnation is merely the result of a fervent wish to be all-inclusive. Or, is it the result of a legitimate interpretation of the Biblical revelation?

1. THE LOGOS CONCEPT AND THE PROLOGUE OF JOHN'S GOSPEL

While it is probably true that Paul has a well-defined logos doctrine in everything but the name, it is the Prologue of John's Gospel that has encouraged the most speculation

concerning the mystery of the incarnation. For our purposes, we are interested only in the question of whether or
not John used the term "logos" with a conscious knowledge
of its philosophical background. Of one thing we can be
certain, namely, that the Prologue ("In the beginning was
the logos . . .") was written in a world where certain metaphysical ideas concerning the logos were common currency.[3]
No approach to this Gospel is valid that does not take this
into account, or ask the question, What did the author hope
and expect his readers would understand from it? From
Heraclitus (ca. 500 B.C.) through Plato and the Stoics, the
term was used to refer to a transmundane reality. From the
Stoics particularly came such important developments as
the idea of the *logos spermatikos,* the seed of reason implanted in every man, which makes immanent the logos,
which permeates the world as a law of nature, making for
order and harmony. There was also a tendency in such works
as the *Hymn of Cleanthes* (ca. 331–232 B.C.) to speak in a
personal way of the Supreme Logos, and to identify the
Sovereign Principle of the Universe with "God most glorious."
This was only a step away from drawing a distinction between this Supreme Deity in his own Being and in his Self-
expression. Interestingly enough, closer to the Christian era,
the logos was often associated with Hermes rather than Zeus
and was conceived after the manner of an avatar in quasi-
human manifestations.

Two factors must also be remembered in thinking about
the Greek background of John's Prologue. One is the Septuagint, in which certain Hebrew words such as *dabhar* were
rendered into Greek by *logos.* For instance, where Ps. 33:6
said that "by the *dabhar* of *yah* were the heavens made," in
the Septuagint this became "by the logos of the Lord were
the heavens made"; or, Ps. 119:89 would read, "Thy logos,
O Lord, endureth forever"; and Ps. 119:105, "Thy logos is
a lamp unto my feet." Commentaries on such passages of

the Septuagint would rely heavily upon Platonic and Stoic ideas. This brings us to the second important factor—the outstanding commentator of the period, Philo, an Alexandrian Jew who was the contemporary of Paul.

One important distinction of the Stoics was to be significant for both Philo and later thinkers: The faculty of reason, as it exists in man, utters itself in speech. Both the faculty and the speech were denoted by the same Greek word, *logos*. The Stoics assigned two attributes to make this distinction. On the one hand, there was the *logos en diathetos* —reason in its inner movement and potentiality. On the other, there was the *logos prophorikos*—reason made concrete in the endless variety of the visible world. Under this distinction, the logos could be both a static concept (the transcendent principle of reason) and a dynamic one (the divine energy of self-revelation). These two meanings of the logos, which were defined in Stoicism, played a much more important role in Philo.

There was a further development in Philo beyond Stoicism. To the Stoics, the principle of reason was ultimate, and there was no necessity of explaining it as the reason of God. It might be described poetically as divine, but this was not a precise meaning. Philo, however, started with the Jewish belief in the supreme self-existing God to whom the creative reason of the world must be related and subordinated. This dilemma, which was to reoccur with greater problems when Christian theologians tried to relate the Son to the Father, accounts for the strange ambivalence of Philo. Sometimes the logos appears as an aspect of the activity of God, at other times as an independent and, it might seem, a personal being.[4] He seems to use the latter concept when speaking of man's enlightenment. The former is his more common expression when he is interested in the cosmic world, both how it came into being and how it is maintained as an intelligible order.

It is not our purpose to develop the ideas current in the world of the Fourth Gospel, but merely to recall them so as to raise the following questions: Was John, as Eric Titus maintains, a literary opportunist, who used a common word of his day for preaching purposes while divorcing it from five hundred years of philosophical development? [5] Or is it almost impossible to think of John's separating his thought so completely from this background? We agree with A. C. Bouquet, the most prominent modern logos theologian who wrestles with the problem of *Religionswissenschaft,* that any educated Gentile, on reading the Prologue, would immediately understand its allusions. Particularly is this so when no explanation of the logos is given, and when almost every verse in it might be paralleled from Philo. [6]

It is not implied, however, that the full gamut of philosophical ideas should be read into John's use of the logos. John has made some radical modifications of the Greek and Jewish backgrounds. For instance, his view of the preexistence of the logos is dominated by his knowledge of its ultimately "becoming flesh." The logos is more than a personification. It has an independent being in relationship to God. Then, the cosmic creativity of the logos—which is so determinative for Philo—is hardly in evidence in John. The only reference is that "all things were made by him." [7] Also, in the Gospel, the term "logos," which can mean either "reason" or "word," means "Word" more than "Reason." It is the reason expressed or revealed, whether that expression is in the person of Jesus himself or that which is uttered by Jesus.

The second important thing to be remembered is that no abstract theory is involved here, such as in the Fathers. It is even relatively unimportant whether, for John, the logos corresponds in all points with Philo's point of view, or with the Wisdom literature of Judaism, for there is no indication that John has thought out the concept with any clearness.

But, when all this is granted, we have still to reckon with the main fact that into the historical tradition of the life and teaching of Jesus a datum is introduced the origin of which is in the thought of the contemporary philosophy. If this is more than a literary device, which we believe it is, then the term "logos" acts like a door that opens the historical event to a transhistorical depth. The word becomes not just a "point of contact" in the first-century world, an accommodation to their thought processes, so to speak, but a suggestion that there is an area in that historical event which will always be bigger than any theological formulation of it. It is this depth to the logos that allows Justin Martyr and William Temple to speak of Christians before the historical Christ. It is also this depth which is serviceable in the modern encounter with world religions.

It is not strange that Hendrik Kraemer should attack this interpretation of the Prologue. We have been arguing for a continuity between the historic Christ and the eternal Christ. Kraemer was emphatic that the relation between the revelation of God in the historic Christ and the truth that might exist in philosophy or world religion was one of radical discontinuity. He maintained that the Prologue was strictly conditioned by Judaism, especially Gen., ch. 1, and Prov., ch. 8. That these latter verses may have been filtered through Philo or the Stoics is not for the moment entertained by Kraemer. It is as if John were presenting purely Jewish ideas, but in a radically new way relating these to the event in Jesus Christ. It was the Fathers who read John in a broad Hellenistic way. They are the culprits, according to Kraemer, who distorted Biblical truth with Greek philosophical concepts. "Our opinion is that the Prologue is, as has already been said, neither philosophy nor mythology nor theology, but a species *sui generis*, rooted in the prophetic Old Testament line." [8]

In order to back up his interpretation, Kraemer seems to

reach out for any likely supporter, including C. H. Dodd
and Rudolf Bultmann. However, his principal defense is
the Biblical theology represented in Kittel's *Theological
Dictionary of the New Testament*, which leads Kraemer to
conclude that, in the Prologue, logos is fundamentally something different from the Hellenistic logos speculation. This
reference to Kittel's work, and the premise of the sharp
distinction between Jewish and Hellenistic thought has been
held up to critical analysis by James Barr in his *Semantics
of Biblical Language*.[9] The work is important for our study
because it points out the shortcomings not only of the *Dictionary*'s use of etymologies but those of Biblical theology in
general. Barr feels that linguistic analysis has often been
used to back up preconceived notions of the difference between Hebrew and Greek mentality. In reacting both to
Biblical criticism and to the comparative study of religions, Biblical theology came to focus on two principles. One
was that Christianity is essentially Jewish, which is a means
of asserting the uniqueness of Christianity. The other is that
there is a common mind among Bible thinkers. This is illus-
trated by the way the contributors to Kittel's *Dictionary*
gather up various meanings of a word and apply them *in
toto* to each particular verse in question. The result is a
Biblical unity, but one that is produced by dogmatic presuppositions rather than by careful linguistic analysis. Barr
probes carefully into the way etymologies are used, and related to concrete statements. Hidden in this usage is very
often a theological game which is played with the etymology,
making it fit the concept of Biblical unity; then, to complete
the game, the stylized etymology is related to concrete Biblical statements in such a way that differences between Biblical authors are minimized.

One case that is very much to the point involves the
article on *mythos* by Stählin in Kittel's *Theological Dictionary of the New Testament*. In this article, logos is set off

from myth, for myth, says Stählin, is rejected by the New Testament.

The Gospel deals with *ta megaleia tou theou*, the mighty acts of God. It is therefore *logos*, historical report of facts, or *prophetikos logos*, prophetic report of facts (cf. II Pet. 1:19). The *mythoi* of erroneous doctrine on the other hand are invented stories, devoid of truth, fables. . . . Logos is the absolutely valid word of God become person; on it everything rests—the faith of the individual and the building of the Church. If the logos is replaced by Myth, then everything is lost; the Word is betrayed.[10]

In contradiction to Stählin, Barr points out other passages, where logos has no reference at all to the historical event. In II Tim. 2:17 for instance, *logos* is used of the ungodly in precisely the same way as the *mythoi* of which we hear elsewhere. There should be, then, says Barr, a suspicion of scholarship that moves from the words of the Bible, not to the thoughts of those who used those words, but to the events themselves or to Christ himself. Then, to call "event" strictly Jewish tradition, whereas "concept" or "idea" is of Greek influence, is to make an artificial distinction. It also ignores the very real problem of what happens when a thought in one language—in this case Hebrew—is brought into a different language of a different culture, i.e., the Greek of the New Testament.

Actually, as has been intimated, no harm is done to the doctrine of the logos by admitting Greek influence upon it. If the logos in the Prologue is not merely a verbal point of contact, but an admission that truth "outside" the historic revelation can be related to the incarnation, this is still not to deny that the enlarged meaning is "the absolutely valid word of God." Sometimes critics of the logos doctrine speak as if by admitting Greek influence upon the logos doctrine the emphasis was shifted to a general principle and away from the incarnate Lord. We are not, however, speaking of a universal logos that can be described with any accuracy

apart from the "Word become flesh." Nor are we implying
any statement of Hindu relativism. The logos is not "separate from," "fuller than," "the source of," the incarnation.
Though logos suggests a principle of rationality, the one who
stands within the theological circle would not know how to
formulate such an interpretation in any abstract terms. To
use any approach like neti neti would deny that specific revelation had occurred in Christ. It is also questionable whether
the term *logos spermatikos* is very useful, in that it is too
easily separated from *logos en sarx*.

Yet, after all attempts to guard against giving an independent status to the logos, the Christian is led by the Prologue up to the edge of a mystery that ultimately escapes
verbal formulation. It is in this sense that Justin Martyr
(and all the succeeding users of the logos idea) cannot with
absolute assurance be sanctioned in his speaking about
"Christians before Christ," but neither can he be denied such
a vision. If there are "Christians before Christ," it must be
affirmed that they are also "Christians in Christ." As one
logos theologian has so aptly put it, "Christ is not only the
historical Christ but also the second person of the trinity,
and the link between God and the world." [11]

Having accepted a legitimate use of the term "logos" in
John, and also in the modern day, we must consider some of
the disadvantages and advantages that are involved in this
position.

2. DISADVANTAGES IN THE LOGOS THEORY

a. *The history of religions must not be stylized.* Once a
logos idea is acknowledged and combined with a faith commitment to Jesus Christ, there is a danger that all the various
elements that *Religionswissenschaft* brings to light will be
placed on some ascending scale that leads up to the incarnation. Implicit in the logos is reason, and it is reason in league
with faith that can force the facts of world religion into a

tidy pattern. This is one of the faults of A. C. Bouquet's study. It seems that he can find traces of the logos everyplace.[12] He remarks, for instance, that though many individual sages emphasize one aspect of "divine Truth," the Christian faith in Jesus Christ "is linked with a recognition of all the many other aspects or facets of the one divine Truth." Thus, he maintains that whereas Hinduism stresses immanence and Islam, transcendence, the Christian faith combines these. This sort of interpretation resists seeing Hinduism and Islam as religions in their own right. There is too quick a desire to bring everything under the umbrella of the logos. Everything becomes grist for the Christian religion in a way that denies dialogue and must anger adherents of other religions. There is also the assumption that the logos, because it has associations with reason, is a completely manageable item, and that faith has given access to its secret. It should be remembered, however, that even in the thought systems of single philosophers there are antinomies. How much more in the structured wholes of living religions.

Much the same criticism could be leveled at R. C. Zaehner. Zaehner sees God revealed "at sundry times and in divers manners," not only in the Old Testament but in other cultures too. Thus Muhammad's emphasis on omnipotence is called "the authentic voice of prophecy." The sacred literature of the Asiatic peoples is "more a *praeparatic evangelica* than Greek philosophy." It was India, says Zaehner, that taught man several things: first of all, that there is one principle that informs both the cosmos and the human soul; secondly, that the human soul is immortal; and finally, that there is a personal God. Zaehner concludes that it is in Christianity that the highest insights of both the Hindus and the Buddhists are fulfilled. Again, the question is raised as to how the logos is known so clearly that it can be the criterion of judgment. Commitment to the theological circle does not necessitate such clarity. In fact, human finiteness and sinfulness rather militate against it. There is the further question as to how isolated elements, in various religions, that are claimed to be part of the logos structure condition the wholes of which they are a part. One of the well-established positions since Kraemer wrote his Tambaram Conference book is that religion should be treated as wholes and not just as a series of dogmas or cultic acts that can be isolated and studied under the microscope. Does the omnipotence of God in Islam, which is claimed as a *kata logon* factor, mean that Islam as a whole is in the path that leads up to the Christian faith? It would be well to heed the words of E. L. Allen, who speaks partly as a philosopher-theologian and partly from his experience as a missionary in China. "The great religions are to be accepted for their own sake and not for the tribute they pay to our religion. What they say to us is not decisive for their work but what they have said to the multitudes who have found shelter and inspiration in them." [13]

However, it is not necessary to disavow the presupposition that there can be found some Christian sense (or logos) in other religions. What is being protested is the neat arranging of religions and not the hope that there is a universal claim in the Christian faith. Some excellent work along these lines has been done by Gerald Cooke in his book *As Christians Face Rival Religions,* which shows that the theologian can do acceptable work in *Religionswissenschaft.* The difference between Cooke and Zaehner or Bouquet is that the antinomies in the religions stand out more clearly in Cooke, leaving the impression that we are dealing with real systems and not just stylized history.

b. *The encounter of religions must not be intellectualized.* This danger is really a continuation of points raised in the other section. Whether logos is taken in either of its meanings, as the reason that orders the world or as the reason that is manifest in it, it is still reason. It is appropriate that the term "logos" be applied to Jesus Christ, whether in preincarnate or incarnate forms. Yet, that which happened in the incarnation is not merely intellectual. Nor is it a confession that we go as far as possible with our intellect, believing that God is Reason even where we cannot comprehend Him. There are tensions in the gospel between Reason and faith, Reason and will, Reason and emotion. The *logos spermatikos*, as a doctrine used in the modern day for keeping Christian theology open to the encounter with world religions, runs the risk of removing these tensions. Paul Lehmann has analyzed this problem very acutely in an article entitled "The Logos in a World Come of Age." [14]

Lehmann notes that in the early church there was a tension in the way the logos was used. Broadly speaking, the logos connected the gospel with the intelligible structure and order of the world and pointed to the intelligibility of the gospel. But, at the same time, the logos connected the gospel concerning Jesus of Nazareth with the self-communication of God as a personal and concrete action—a revelatory relation. The tension between personal relationship and rational principle is seen in the fact that whereas the New Testament has few references to the logos and whereas the logos was not used in the ecumenical creeds of the church, classical theology found the term indispensable. "Apparently," says Lehmann, "the formative factor in this theological preoccupation was the Prologue of John's Gospel. Its eloquence and force were such as to have overcome the curious reticence of Scripture and creed in relating logos to Gospel."

Now, says Lehmann, in a world come of age, the relation of gospel to logos has fallen into disrepair. "The laboriously forged link between soteriology and intelligibility, which once and for a long time gave the shape of words to the Gospel, has been shattered in and by a world from which God is effectively absent." The problem, says Lehmann, is not God's actual absence, but rather the breakdown of the language and the sense for transcendence that the early church had. "The difference between a world come of age and a world initially surprised by the advent of the logos, is that in a world come of age the logos must create new conditions for the experience and apprehension of transcendence, and not merely correct conditions already at hand." Theology in this day has a continuing task of describing and sustaining a creative relation between soteriology and intelligibility.

Yet, Lehmann notes, this task for theology is not an easy one, because a "fateful inversion" took place in the early centuries. The apostolic fathers tried to give the shape of words to the gospel by means of the logos without seeing the tension of the relation. The gospel of Jesus the logos became the gospel of the logos in Jesus. The logos became the bearer of truth, a principle of reason, rather than the embodiment of grace and truth. The outcome was that the logos doctrine, which was originally designed to give an appropriate shape of words to the gospel, actually functioned to distort the communication and interpretation of the gospel. Or, to paraphrase Dietrich Bonhoeffer, "the logos doctrine has actually functioned to repress rather than to attest to the anti-logos at whose insistence the doctrine was initially included in the theological response of the church to the self-identifying, self-communication of God to man and the world in Jesus Christ." [15] It must be remembered that the gospel liberates the logos, and not vice versa.

Such a danger of the logos distorting the gospel, which Lehmann has pointed out, is revealed in many ways in the encounter of world religions. One example among many others is the thesis of the Roman Catholic scholar, J. A. Cuttat.[16] Cuttat uses logos theology as an invitation to a mystical experience, but the result seems to be an intellectual exercise in which the other religions are subsumed under Christianity in much the same way as was pointed out in the previous section.

For Cuttat, the comparison of religions can be a "providential invitation" to one adherent of a religion to review his own doctrine so as to rediscover potential dimensions within it. What this means for the Christian is that he must see his faith as wide enough to receive other faiths, while other faiths will only make sense to their adherents by being subsumed under Christianity. Cuttat uses Radhakrishnan as his foil. The latter's universalism is based on man's capacity to transcend himself by entering into himself. Also, this transcendency of himself leads to a divine who is One, but known by many names. But, says Cuttat, following Coomaraswamy, Radhakrishnan rejects revelation, which is the essence of Christianity, and is so tolerant that he admits that truth can never be known. Instead of a universal religion that rests on truth, Radhakrishnan has succumbed, according to Cuttat, to a basically European idea of evolution which has no basis in any sacred writing, including his own. "We will endeavor to show," says our author, "without using the path of logic, or resorting to the authority of dogma, that the metaphysical perspective cannot subordinate the monotheistic viewpoint without eventually depriving it of its essential elements—personal transcendence, gratuitousness of Grace, the supreme value of love—whereas monotheistic revelation is capable of embracing the Eastern perspective, in such a way that the true essence of the latter is not only preserved, but heightened." [17] How compelling this "logic" is to a Hindu is questionable. But it is on this basis of monotheism over monism that Cuttat turns the quest for unity into a very simple system. Beginning with mysticism, he analyzes the meaning of this experience. He uses the term "interiority" to describe the mystical act, rather than "introspection," since the mystic's aim is to transcend subjectivism and reach God. Introspection connotes too much the idea of the psychiatrist's couch. In mysticism, Western or Oriental, self-transcendence takes place. Carry mystical discipline as far as you will, allowing the Orient to help in methodology and finally, at the end of human effort, God must break through. "To go to the ontological core of being is to wait to meet God." But—and the dogmatic logic noted above is evident—it is the transcendent God, the Other, who is met. This transcendent God is always meeting the Oriental mys-

tic, says Cuttat, whether he knows it or not. He might phi-
losophize about the experience in terms of monism, but this
is where he needs the schooling of Christianity.

The theory that gives Cuttat his confidence that the Oriental is meeting a personal God is based on the incarnation
of Jesus Christ. Christ unites "full interiority and absolute
transcendency." He fulfills the deepest non-Christian intuitions. There is not something universal about the incarnation
in the sense that God became *a man*. Rather, God in Christ
is God in humanity, and all history is affected. History is
now sacred history. The true mystical experience anyplace
is then possible through the incarnation that occurred distinctively in Jesus Christ. The latter is God's infinite power
within man's reach.

The mystery of the incarnate logos is a fascinating theme.
It allows Cuttat to look for suggestions of it every place,
much after the manner of Bouquet and Zaehner. He is much
enamored with the idea that "Pure Land" Buddhism arose
at the time of Christ's birth. This is to him more than a coincidence. He interprets Ramanuja's Bhakti theology in the
same way. Ramanuja's idea, that the God-creature polarity
must lead to the Wholly Other or else his presence is lost, is
simply a natural man's straining after Christian revelation.
Zen Buddhism, which stresses so strongly the disparity between human effort and spiritual "answer," and also of
"letting go" to the fullest extent, is really close to what Christians call grace. Such a broad interpretation of the incarnation, as Cuttat gives, allows a Christian to become God-
intoxicated, Western-style, and certainly helps him see the
relevance of the Christian faith, providing he can accept the
dogmatic base.

However, what is objectionable in Cuttat's analysis is
that he is so confident that he understands the way the logos
is working. It is at this point that the tension which Lehmann emphasized is gone. The result is a highly intellectualized Christianity coupled with a dogmatic appeal for the

non-Christian religions to submit to Jesus Christ. "That which is absolutely impossible to the human will's ascending toward God has become infinitely possible through the divine will's descent toward man, *on the one essential condition that man accept unreservedly this new dispensation*." [18] This seems to involve Cuttat in a logical impasse. On the one hand, according to him, numbers of non-Christians have been having a valid, though unconscious, encounter with the personal God; yet on the other hand, this encounter is not really possible at all unless these non-Christians accept the theory of it. However, Cuttat does not seem bothered by this paradox. While the need for conversion to Christianity is not stressed in the book, conversion should follow logically from the true insight into the nature of the mystical experience. It is axiomatic for Cuttat that "none can pass from the interiority of the heart to the 'abyss of the Father' save through the Son."

Here we will arrest our discussion of Cuttat. He points up the very real danger of intellectualizing the incarnation to the point where mystery has been swallowed up by knowledge. The Christian theologian, even where he is attracted to mysticism, is never free to give the impression that the experience is a packaged commodity within the limits of the human mind. In one sense "we know"; in another sense "we see through a glass darkly." The very confrontation with the logos, a confrontation that begs to be put into thought and speech, does at the same time confound all efforts at complete communication.

c. *Contrary evidence must not be omitted.* One of the important authors who writes as a Christian theologian, and with the awareness of *Religionswissenschaft* is Ernst Benz, professor of church history at the University of Marburg. In his several writings on the theology of the history of religions, he is quite insistent that a logos doctrine cannot handle the contrary facts that have been brought to light in the modern era.[19] The first contrary fact is the new understanding of how old the human race is. Formerly, says Benz, the logos doctrine operated within a limited segment of history. According to the Byzantine imperial church, Christ was born in the year 5509, the number of years from the creation of the world! It was relatively easy to order such a segment of history, bringing the heathen world into an alliance with the people of God through the covenant of Noah, and having it all coming to fulfillment with Jesus Christ. What of prehistory? Benz asks. Then, too, there is the fact that new religions keep appearing *post Christum,* and old ones are more vital than ever. For instance, in 1957 there were a total of 377 religious groups registered with the government in Japan. In the postwar resurgence, 700 new religions had registered. About half disappeared after the enforcement of the new Religious Corporation Law of 1951, but others made remarkable advances. At least five of them have won more than 600,000 adherents each. Reiyukai alone, a Nichiren sect, has gained a membership of 2,300,000, or more than four times the total Christian population. Apparently there is no growing appreciation for the Christian faith; rather, the opposition to Christianity has been intensified. These are the contrary facts that Benz feels cannot be handled by the logos doctrine. The solution Benz proposes is a theology in which love is emphasized, rather than any dogma such as the logos. It is love, and not doctrine, insists Benz, that relates the contrary evidence to salvation history.

There are several criticisms that would apply to Benz. One is that he seems to identify logos theology with an exclusivist view of Christianity. He also sees the doctrine as valid only if there is some observable historic connection between religions and epochs and the Christian era; or, if there is some observable historical fulfillment in Christianity. All these, however, are limitations that are imposed on the logos. But what is most objectionable is that Benz proposes to relate non-Christian faith to salvation history by the category of love. If this love is independent of the logos, then it is operating in the same way as philosophical ideas operated in the "first great stage" of *Religionswissenschaft*. If, contrary to this, Benz's category of love is kept in the Godhead, then basically he has not left the logos position. All he has said, which is not a great advancement, is that there is a danger of forgetting that agape is involved in the logos, whether *en arché* or *en sarx*. He has said this in a dangerous way, however, unless a Feuerbachian philosophy is advocated. For, while there is no objection to saying God is Love, there is a great objection to making the predicate into the subject, as Feuerbach did.

In the same collection of essays to which Benz has contributed, there is a helpful suggestion by Paul Devanandan that tries to account for the vitality of non-Christian religions in relation to the logos. After making a case that God in Christ is active universally, in religions other than our own, he reminds us that what we have termed "contrary evidence" is not merely to be found in the non-Christian world. Quoting from a report of a group of Christian leaders in India, he says: "There is indeed a frontier, but it does not lie between the Christian man and the non-Christian man, but within both. . . . For we, in large measure, are heathen still. We need to be converted as does the Hindu." [20] This recognition has the advantage of undercutting the sharp division Benz makes between the Christian revelation and the facts of the non-Christian world that cannot be adjusted to that revelation. There is a frontier at the heart of the Christian faith as well as at the periphery. Devanandan's conclusion is as follows: He asks whether the preaching of the gospel is legitimately directed to the total annihilation of all religions other than Christianity. He does not feel this should be the case, but believes that God is involved eschatologically in "radical renewal," in all religions, Christianity included.

d. *Secularization must not be "controlled."* One of the

greatest obstacles to any reworking of the logos theme is the modern realization that the world is a secular world. In the 1928 meeting of the International Missionary Conference at Jerusalem, secularism was declared an enemy of the church, and Christians were urged by some leaders to unite with other faiths so as to combat it. This was a Toynbee-like approach, and was not necessarily hostile to a logos theology.[21] Since the last world war, and particularly through the influence of Bonhoeffer, this treatment of profane existence will no longer do. Bonhoeffer spoke of secularization[22] as a liberation: "the abandonment of a false concept of God and the clearing of the decks for the God of the Bible."

Since Bonhoeffer announced this *Weltanschauung,* there have been a variety of ways in which a theology of secularization has developed. One very helpful analysis of the contemporary scene describes two main types of secular theology.[23] Right-wing radicals, such as John Robinson and Harvey Cox, are more concerned with communication than with the content of the gospel. With them, the emphasis is on new theological statement and institutional forms. The left-wing radicals, such as Altizer, Hamilton, and van Buren, feel that Christianity's dialectic between transcendence and immanence has collapsed. For the left wing, history is the incarnation of God's self-expression and self-fulfillment. The polarity between the sacred and profane is said to be dissolved, with the only possibility being a nonreligious world and a nonreligious faith. In left-wing theology, logos statements are nonsense statements, for a radical interpretation is placed upon the death of God. By "death of God," these scholars do not mean (1) that God is there for faith but not for theology (Bultmann); or (2) that God is there as being-itself, but not as *a* being (Tillich); or (3) that God is there as radically immanent, but not as a transcendent being. God is not there at all. "He" is ruled out as personal being, metaphysical structure, or primordial ground.

If the left-wing type of radical theology is chosen, then it is hard to see how any logos position is possible. However, if the door is open for metaphysics at all, such as is implicit in the right-wing radical group, then the reverse is true. As Kleever observes, "metaphysical grounding may not refer to a 'realm,' but 'confessionally' may point to structures of reality in which our whole range of facts cohere." Without arguing this point, nor entering into the modern discussion of secularization, we are assuming that the right wing is a defensible position in which secularization can be taken seriously along with a logos Christology. This is what Tillich and Eliade attempted to do.

One theologian, however, deserves special consideration, since secularization is the cornerstone of his system. This is Arend Van Leeuwen, whose book *Christianity in World History*[24] has caused a great amount of discussion in mission circles. Oddly enough, Van Leeuwen sees secularization as a positive outgrowth of Christianity, and is indebted to Bonhoeffer, though he shows no familiarity with either the right- or left-wing American theologians, Tillich included. Van Leeuwen's thought is developed in a massive way, with illustrations from Biblical theology, cultural anthropology, and the history of religions. Briefly put, his thesis is this: There are two basic types of civilization, the theocratic and the ontocratic. The latter has been combined with religion from primitive times. In the ontocratic civilization, the world and God form a cosmic whole. The movement of history today, however, is against this pattern. Since the industrial revolution, the world has become more and more free to be manipulated and controlled by man, completely divorced from any control by God. This irreversible movement of history toward secularization was born in the West, and is spreading all over the world. The important point Van Leeuwen wants to make is that the process toward secularization cannot be rightly and properly weighed unless one realizes that the vital impulse behind it comes from the Biblical message. His constant theme is that this secularization will break down all religions, including any attempt to revive a *Corpus Christianum*. Since, however, Christianity gave birth to the technological age and is necessary to understand the history through which the world is moving at this time, then the acceptance of its gospel should follow in the wake of the tremendous revolution that is taking place. What Christianity was not able to do in a frontal assault by evangelism, it may be able to do when it comes incognito in modern technology. This thesis of Van Leeuwen has overtones of the nineteenth century, particularly Ritschl's emphasis that the gospel and civilization are tied. The difference is that Van Leeuwen is conscious of the judgment that the gospel places upon empirical Christianity. In this he is at one with Hendrik Kraemer, who incidentally writes the foreword to his book.

The "Biblical realism" of Van Leeuwen is seen in Chs. 2 and 3 of *Christianity in World History,* where he attempts to show that Israel's history was different from all other histories. Israel persistently refused the enticements of mysticism and would not admit the claims of the logos upon her. The state, the kingship, and the Temple were not sacralized as in other religions. Instead, there was a radical split between earth and the kingship of God. One myth that is crucial for Van Leeuwen is that of the tower of Babel. This picture of the attempt to tie heaven and earth, and divinize the whole of life, is at the heart of ontocracy. Yet the attempt failed. The significance of the failure is that the secular world was allowed to exist in freedom, though the freedom has only been realized in our times. The problem with today is that the secular city, which is free by divine fiat, is still haunted by the frustration that it cannot reach to the heavens. That is why the secular city must understand its roots in the Bible and listen anew to the church's proclamation.

What is the impact of secularization on the non-Western world? Van Leeuwen vacillates between agnosticism and optimism. At times he says that we will have to wait and see.

At other times, he feels this is the greatest day Christianity ever had, as when he quotes Carl F. von Weizsäcker: "Today, secularized modern society is subduing the non-Christian world which missions have not been able to subdue. Apparently, the step to its secularized and therefore isolated content is easier than the complete transfer to Christianity. Yet the two go together and the consequences of secularism confronts us forceably with the Christian question." [25] In any event, Van Leeuwen is certain that Christian missions do not have to be embarrassed by an intrinsic tie to Western technology, since it is impossible for the church to be divorced from a world that is being revolutionized by Western culture. Even K. M. Panikkar, who holds that the Christian mission is a failure because it made claims for the uniqueness of European culture, nonetheless admits that the West brought a "qualitative break" in the history of Asia that has affected "their religious and philosophical systems, the material set-up of their lives and mental outlook . . . to an extent which is not possible for anyone to estimate now." [26] Such an admission is enough for Van Leeuwen to claim that a line has been crossed not only in the West but throughout the world. The history of the world is confronted with a full-scale invasion by technology, which cannot be dodged until the relentless transformation is accomplished. The church must interpret this history "until the invading history is no longer suffered as blind process . . . but that men can determine in it the voice of Christ and those of counterfeits."

Some observations are in order concerning this condensed presentation of Van Leeuwen's thought. At first, his positive evaluation of secularization seems hostile to any logos idea. He himself includes the logos as an illustration of ontocracy. It is, he maintains, a static concept of reality, the object of theoretical, impersonal knowledge. It is part of the primitive, mystical mentality in which subject and object are one —the logos as the essential objective order of reality corresponding to an analogous logos in the knowing subject (cf. Tillich). By contrast, he maintains that the Hebrew *dabhar* "is dynamic, and arises from a relationship between the one who speaks the word and the one who hears." This radical distinction which Van Leeuwen makes between the Greek logos and the Hebrew *dabhar* is why there is such a kinship between Van Leeuwen and Barth and Kraemer. However, one important difference is this. The ponderous "no" that Barth hears spoken against man in his religion, which judges all human systems, comes from the Wholly Other. The "no" that Van Leeuwen hears comes from the irresistible movement of world history and secularization.

However, it is at this point that a couple of criticisms might be directed against Van Leeuwen. Is it possible, in a day when the "death of God" theology has questioned all meaning given to the words "God" and "transcendence," for any man to write in complete unawareness of this dialogue? Furthermore, is there no distinction in the way logos might be used? The logos of Greek philosophy, which was used by the Fathers to handle the problem of the One and the Many, or to handle the problem of explaining the Christ, might be a lot closer to ontocracy than the logos used by a man like Eliade, and called by him "the Sacred." In the first case the emphasis is on intelligibility, and the modern world has broken down this use of the logos. We can no longer look at our world as if everything were explained and controlled by a metaphysical principle. But if we use the logos as a way of describing soteriology—"The light which lighteth every man"—then the term might not be far from the dynamic use of *dabhar*. The Christian confession would then be that the movement of enlightenment is always a gracious act of the Christ which occurs in ontocratic and theocratic societies. We do not see, therefore, that Van Leeuwen's thesis need be against any use of the logos concept.

The bigger question, as to what effect secularization will have on all the world religions, and how Christianity itself

will be affected in its mission, is not convincingly handled by
Van Leeuwen. It is hard to believe that the renascent world
religions will fall before secularism without some reconception that Van Leeuwen would still call ontocracy.[27] It is also
hard to see just what Van Leeuwen is directing the church
to do in these times. His last chapter is highly disappointing.
There is a call to understand the technological revolution,
namely, that secularism was made possible by the Christian
civilization itself. We are, therefore, called upon to cooperate
with the forces breaking away from the fetters of sacred
tradition. Yet this is nothing new. It is not much of an advance over the Laymen's Report of 1932. Therefore the
general conclusion from reading Van Leeuwen's book is that
it is a brilliant attempt to show the Biblical roots of secularism, but that the concrete proposals addressed to the
church in the light of this analysis are not clear. This is why
the encounter of world religions must go on in the midst of
the current theological discussion of the meaning of secularity. What is hoped is that in the tendency in East and
West to assert the autonomy of man and the world, there
might still be a variety of ways to encounter what some have
called "The Great Secular Man" and with what we have
call the logos.

3. THE VALUES OF THE LOGOS DOCTRINE

Admitting there are dangers involved in logos theology,
we acknowledge that there are also some real values. In each
case to be mentioned, it is the openness of the Christian faith
in the encounter with world religions that is at stake. Let us
consider these briefly:

a. *Exclusivist Bible verses can be deepened.* If the Biblical
witness to God's Word is accepted, there are statements that
apparently have restrictive meaning, and that would limit
revelation to the historic event in Jesus Christ. Some of these
verses are:

No one knows the Father except the Son and any one to whom
the Son chooses to reveal him. (Matt. 11:27; cf. Luke 10:22.)

I am the way, and the truth, and the life; no one comes to the
Father, but by me. (John 14:6.)

And there is salvation in no one else, for there is no other name
under heaven given among men by which we must be saved. (Acts
4:12.)

Such verses as these seem to teach that only those who
consciously profess faith in the historic Jesus Christ can
have a saving knowledge of God; so that logically all un-
converted non-Christians, as well as the religious systems to
which they belong, must be regarded as outside the way of
salvation.

There are several ways to react to this exclusivist train of
thought. Some can deny the veracity of such verses, either by
employing Biblical criticism as a weeding tool or else by a
more frank refusal to admit the witness of these verses. For
instance, Floyd Ross acknowledges that the early Christians
did put forth the claim that "there is no other name. . . ."
But, with candor, he admits: "That the early Christians may
have been over-zealous in stating it in this way is a possibility the Christian must live with." [28] Ross himself tries to
distinguish between confessional statements and historical
statements. Acts 4:12 would be classed as confessional in
that it relates to man's inner response. By historical, Ross
means the ordinary usage of that term, involving the methods of historiography and the attempt to establish the occur-
rence or nonoccurrence of objective events. The damage is
done, according to Ross, when we speak of the mythic or
confessional as if it were literal or historical. Yet it might be
argued, in reverse, whether Ross has not dissolved *Historie*
into some form of self-understanding (just as Bultmann has
done), which is then labeled "confessional." It is because
of the unimportance that he attaches to history that he sees
the Hindu doctrine of avatara and the Christian doctrine of

incarnation as not too far removed from each other.

If Ross's alternative to the exclusivist passages of Scripture be rejected, if we are not willing to say that early Christians may have been overzealous, there remains the possibility of balancing "open" passages with exclusivist ones. For instance:

I have existed before Abraham was born. (John 8:58, Moffatt.)
The Logos of Life . . . existed with the Father and was disclosed to us. (I John 1:2, Moffatt.)

This is not how you have understood the meaning of Christ . . .
—the real Christ who is in Jesus. (Eph. 4:20-21, Moffatt.)

They [Israel] drank of that spiritual Rock that followed them: and that Rock was Christ. (I Cor. 10:4, KJV.)

It might be argued that there are antinomies in the Bible's teaching about Jesus Christ, of the same sort as the predestination/free will controversy. Therefore, since Jesus Christ is presented both from an exclusivist and from an open point of view, an option is given as to which side is stressed. Once again, as in the first argument, the desire is to avoid Acts 4:12 rather than to face it squarely.

It is the value of logos theology, however, to consider every reference to the historical Jesus Christ and to realize that depths are indicated that can be caught up in no clear-cut statement of faith. In other words, all the verses quoted above as open passages are not to be laid over against a set of verses that are exclusivist, as if some contradiction existed. Rather, it is the open verses that add mystery and suggestiveness to the exclusivist ones, just as it is the exclusivist texts that prevent the freer logos interpretation from dissolving into sheer sentimentality.[29] For the Christian, commitment to Jesus Christ is inextricably bound to the logos *en sarx*. As revealed in the Scriptures, as constantly confronting us, Jesus Christ is the window through which we see the enormity of his revelation. We are even committed to the belief that without that window we may see nothing at all. Yet, we need not assume that the challenge of the logos *en sarx* will cut exactly along the lines that divide "the church" (as we see it) from "the world."

b. *Exclusivist adjectives can be broadened.* There are certain adjectives that circle around the revelation of God in Christ, such as "complete," "exhaustive," "final," "absolute." Such adjectives are very properly used of Jesus Christ, and yet they have a variety of senses in which they can be taken. Some of these senses are exclusivist, and others are open.

For instance, when it is said that the revelation of Jesus Christ is "complete," does this mean "complete as I know it in my historical situation," "complete as I may someday know it in my historical situation," "complete in history apart from any worshiper's value judgment," or "complete only *en sarx* and *en archē*"? The first two ways of taking the adjective "complete" are certainly more exclusivist in tendency than the last two. They are also the meanings usually given when Christianity is called complete. For instance, at the Jerusalem Missionary Conference of 1928, Robert E. Speer put it as follows: "There is no truth anywhere which is not in Christ, and in Christ in its fullest and richest form. . . . Not only are all the truths of the other religions in Christianity, but they are balanced and corrected as they are not in the non-Christian religions." [30] And again, in a section entitled "These Values Not a Supplement to Christianity," Speer continues: "What the other religions forget, or never knew, Christianity tells us in the fullness of its truth." [31] It is obvious that by "Christ," Speer means the historic Jesus, and by "Christianity" he means the historical religion that has sprung from him. If this is the only statement of the case, then the word "complete" will retain a narrow meaning. But as soon as some meaning is given to *en archē*, the adjective "complete" shifts its meaning.

Let us grant that the whole of God's Word (his self-expression to man), all truth so far made known to man, is contained in Jesus Christ. But, even granting this, are the terms "Jesus," "Christ," "the Word of God," and "God" all interchangeable in meaning? Even the New Testament witness does not say this, as for instance, "My Father is greater than I" (John 14:28) or " The Son [shall] be subject unto him that put all things under him, that God may be all in all" (I Cor. 15:28). It is therefore essential to distinguish between the total Word, or self-expression, of God—which must surely be conceived as perfect—and the historic revelation in Jesus. The Report of the Archbishop's Commission, *Doctrine in the Church of England,* pointed out the subordinate characteristics of the historic Christ. "Nor is it to be maintained that every sort of human excellence is found in Christ. His mission was that of Messiah, not that (for example) of a statesman or of an artist. . . . There is no reason to attribute to Him the excellences appropriate to functions that were not his." [32] As Dewick concludes, "If we are not to expect to find in Jesus 'every sort of human excellence,' *a fortiori,* we shall not expect to find in Him all the infinite attributes of the Divine; and in that case, the revelation of God in Him cannot be a complete revelation." [33] All of this is not to disparage or minimize the historic revelation in Jesus Christ. For the Christian there is no fuller or deeper truth than in him. Yet it is possible to believe this, and still approach the non-Christian religions with an open mind that has not rejected, on a priori grounds, the possibility that these religions may contribute to our knowledge of God, and that they may bring to light for us elements of the logos that we have not detected in its historic manifestation.

A similar argument might be used concerning the word "final" as it relates to the historic revelation in Jesus Christ. Does it mean "a once-for-all happening" or "a once-for-all meaning concerning that which happened"? And, what is the relation of the latter to my historical and ever-changing time? As Heraclitus states, we cannot take a step into the same river twice. What does it mean to say that I, who am part of the changing structure of things, apprehend that which is a "once-for-all event"? If it takes two to make a revelation, as we have said elsewhere, can the word "final" be used of Jesus Christ without including my apprehension of Jesus Christ? If there is no way of using the term "final" apart from my apprehension, does this not change the meaning of "final" by surrounding it with my own relative posture?

There is some help in answering these questions by defining the word "final" in such a way that it avoids a head-on clash between the eternal and the temporal. For instance, Tillich uses the term "final" in an existential way. For Tillich, "final revelation" means more than *the last,* or genuine, revelation. It means the decisive, fulfilling, unsurpassable revelation, which is the criterion of all others. Or, to take a different approach, Dewick calls Jesus Christ "final" in the sense of "completely satisfying." Such definitions have the advantage of keeping the Christian revelation anchored to the historic event while at the same time accounting for the ever-changing present in which I view that event.

One of the great fears of mission leaders has been that if the word "final" were tampered with in any way, we would be victims of an erosive relativism. Kraemer, for instance, speaks of the modern world as being under the victorious but dreadful dominion of relativism, which lies like an "abyss" before mankind today.[34] However, relativism can mean that nothing is final in relation to anything else; that all roads up the mountain are equally good (assuming that there is a mountain in the first place). This meaning of relativism is denied. For the Christian, God was in Christ, and this is decisive. However, we also use relativism to indicate the fact that in all human judgments and thinking there is the element of imperfection which can never be eliminated. We know the Absolute relatively.

c. *Christian appreciation can be widened.* The type of fulfillment theory advocated by J. N. Farquahr in his classic
book *The Crown of Hinduism* can no longer stand up in an
age that has felt the influence of *krisis* theology. At the
same time, in the contact between Christian faith and non-
Christian faith, there should be many testimonies by theologian and common lay person to the all-inclusive nature of the
logos.

The testimony of converts to the Christian faith is often
intense on either side of the question, How do you see your
former religion? Such surveys of the converted, however,
have their limitations. The understanding of our past is not
always the keenest in the first flush of conversion, but rather
after years of growth and of mature theological insight. If
logos theology is correct, we should expect to find from
Christian biography that the maturity of Christian experience, represented by the devout, leads to a greater appreciation of the best in the non-Christian experience. For instance, Kitagawa likened Buddhism to the ninth resting
place on the ascent to Mt. Fuji (almost to the top). Likewise, A. J. Appasamy tells of the experience of his father, a
Christian pastor, who late in his life returned more and
more to the practice of yoga. Such experiences could be multiplied. In fact, there is an interesting suggestion of A. C.
Bouquet, which he makes in several of his writings, that it
might not be impossible for there to be Christian Buddhists,
Christian Muslims, Christian Vedantists, etc., in the same
sense that in the past there have been Christian Platonists
and Aristotelians and Stoics.[35] The seriousness of Bouquet's
proposal will depend, among other things, on the doctrine of
the church and its Sacraments. Certainly, though, there is not
in the Orient the same pattern of identifying with churches
and denominations as there is in the West. Be that as it
may, there should be some weight given to the testimony of
converts from non-Christian religions. If there is the logos
en archē, as we believe, then a growing appreciation by the

converts of their heritage as well as their newfound faith might be expected. They would then be agreeing with Paul, "For all things are yours; whether Paul, or Apollos, or Cephas, or the world, or life, or death, or things present, or things to come; all are yours; and ye are Christ's; and Christ is God's" (I Cor. 3:21–23).

From a slightly different perspective, the logos idea—though not named as such—has been the basis of a new look at the evangelistic approach to other faiths. One book, which was recently commissioned by the Department of Missionary Studies of the World Council of Churches, is D. T. Niles's *Upon the Earth*. When Niles speaks of the resurgent religions and the church's response to them, he says: "In meeting this thrust of the religions, however, the demand upon the Church is not simply that it should be aware of the nature of the uniqueness of its own faith. That is paramount. But it is fruitless unless there goes with it the willingness and the ability to see all men in Christ, even men in their religions, so that seeing them thus one may converse with them about their Saviour." [36] This idea that Christ is to be found in all human activities and in our brother on the road—what some call Christ's prevenience, but which is really a logos theology—was much discussed at New Delhi in 1961. However, it is not just a theme of the last decade. W. E. Hocking records an interview that he had with a great missionary to India, C. F. Andrews. Hocking asked Andrews whether he had been trying to convert Indians to Christianity. He replied: "I always assume that they *are* Christians; and after I have talked with them for a while, I sometimes see the light of Christ coming into their eyes." [37]

Such a view of the evangelistic task is often coupled with a doctrine of universalism. Niles entertains this doctrine, but does not commit himself, since he acknowledges the possibility of damnation. More interesting for our present purposes is Karl Barth, since his thought underlies Kraemer's theology at so many points. What is often overlooked is that

Barth comes as close as possible to universalism, though rejecting the use of this term.

Just to feel the contrast in his thinking, a quote from his "Questions to Christendom" of 1928 will suffice.

Does Christendom know how near to her lies the temptation by a slight betrayal of her proper business, to escape such an imminent conflict with these alien religions? Does she know that this must not happen? We can only ask, Does she know that under no circumstances must she howl with the wolves? . . . Christendom should advance right into the midst of the "religions," whatever their names may be, and let come what will, deliver her message of the one God and of His compassion for men forlorn, without yielding by a hairbreadth to their "daemons." [38]

In his later book, *The Humanity of God,* the climate is quite changed. In this book he admits that the pendulum of his emphasis needed to swing back. In the aftermath of nineteenth-century anthropocentric theology, "humanity" needed the fierce "no." Barth says that at that time it was necessary to use phrases such as "wholly other," "perpendicularly from above," "infinite qualitative distinction." Anything of mysticism, morality, pietism, and romanticism had to be cleared away. Now, says Barth, we must see that the deity of the living God finds its meaning in the context of his history and his dialogue with man and in his togetherness with men. In Jesus Christ is the history, the dialogue in which God and man meet and are together. On behalf of God, Jesus Christ calls; on behalf of man, he intercedes. "God's deity is no prison in which He can exist only in and for Himself; but in Jesus Christ He has the high freedom to love."

Important consequences follow from this premise. One is that man's culture gains distinction. It is man's attempt to be man, says Barth, and to hold the gift of his humanity in honor. But—and here is the tremendous change of emphasis —the kerygma is not addressed to those who are "outsiders" to God's grace. They are all "insiders" who are not yet awakened.[39]

In this context Barth makes his observation concerning universalism. The theologian must be positive and say "no" to the transgression of man. But God in Christ takes the "no" to himself and is the victor. Therefore, Barth claims that human nature is naturally Christian. Barth ties this in with Col. 1:20, that Jesus Christ is "to reconcile all things unto himself," and suggests that while he still does not want to label this universalism, we should not be panicked by the word, nor should we ever set limits on God's loving-kindness. Barth is not writing this with world religions in mind, though the application to the encounter is obvious. While Kraemer does not follow this line of Barth's theology, it means that for Barthians who do, the old distinction between continuity and discontinuity has been transcended. This too was put forth as one of the values of logos theology.

IV

The Experience of the Logos

In the preceding chapter, the caution was raised that an acceptance of some form of logos Christology might lead to a stylized history of religions. That is, there is always the danger, to which all logos theologians are susceptible, of trying to explain all contrary religious facts and fit them into an intelligible pattern. This we are not at liberty to do. It may be that future dialogue will produce mutual understanding and an obvious movement of history toward a reconceived Christianity. For this to be so, there would have to be an acknowledgment by adherents of other religions that the logos *en archē* is also the logos *en sarx*; or else an acknowledgment by Christian theologians that the logos *en archē* is more central to the Christian faith than the logos *en sarx*. Neither admission is likely, and all historical evidence shows that other religions are moving farther away from Christianity, and revitalizing their own missionary drive.

However, there is an area supported by logos Christology that is open to investigation—and this is the area of religious experience. If doctrine, cult, and historic origins, *Weltanschauungs,* and so forth, have infinite variety and contradiction, what about religious experience? To posit the logos *en archē* by theology suggests a hypothesis that can be tested by phenomenology. The test can never be a proof of the logos, but merely an affirmation that is consistent with logos Christology. In this connection, we will consider Rudolf Otto, together with some theologians of religious experience.

In the next chapter, we will consider Paul Tillich's theology of ultimate concern. The main difference of approach in these two chapters is that Tillich works consciously under the theological norm and has given a theological statement of the norm that applies to psychological experience. Otto is more the phenomenologist.

It is interesting that Otto was led to his phenomenological investigation by his Christian commitment—particularly his interpretation of Luther's concept of the *Deus absconditus*. This doctrine of Luther discussed in his *The Bondage of the Will*, was largely ignored by the Ritschlian school as a medieval aberration. For Ritschl, the revelation of God in Jesus Christ was adequate for man, and the thought of God's hiddenness had little religious value. This neglect of the *Deus absconditus* concept, both by Ritschl and the Ritschlian movement, as well as by the wave of Luther interpreters of the late nineteenth and early twentieth centuries, was rejected by Rudolf Otto. In his book *The Idea of the Holy* (*Das Heilige*), he mentions the *Deus absconditus* only twice, but in both cases it reveals an essential tie between Luther's insight and his own analysis of religious experience. The point we wish to make is this: *If* there can be an analysis of Christian experience such as Otto made—assuming it is the kerygma that produced this experience—and *if* an analysis of non-Christian religious experience shows the same elements as the Christian analysis, a pointer is set up toward a broader (or deeper) interpretation of the Christian revelation. Otto's two books dealing with the Christian faith and the two main branches of Hinduism—Vedanta and Bhakti—are illustrative of an encounter that the theologian could say is possible because of his theological commitment to the logos *en archē*.[1]

Tillich's approach is far different, though leading to the same basis for religious encounter. Tillich is a philosopher-theologian who happens to be concerned with religious experience among other things. When he begins his philosophical discussion of "Reason and Revelation," he speaks of "the depth of reason."

The depth of reason is the expression of something that is not reason but which precedes reason and is manifest through it. Reason in both its objective and its subjective structures points to something which appears in these structures but which transcends them in power and meaning.[2]

Tillich realizes that any term used to describe the depth of reason must of necessity be metaphorical. Terms such as "substance," "being-itself," "ground," and "abyss" are all possibilities.[3] He himself has used "ground of being" because of its metaphorical and logical power, while preferring the classical scholastic term of *esse ipsum* (being-itself).[4] But, in any case, what is indicated is the "depth" of reason, which is essentially manifest in reason itself. It is a form of the *Deus absconditus,* used in a very different way from Luther,[5] and yet belonging in the same family of ideas.

Tillich is of special concern in our study because more than any other of the leading existentialist thinkers, he has actively engaged in the encounter of world religions as a Christian theologian. We will be concerned with how he engages in this encounter, and more particularly with whether or not he has kept his commitment to the revelation in Jesus Christ in the process of doing it. Tillich has a broad base to his theology in which he would like to say, contrary to Pascal, that the God of the philosophers *is* the God of Abraham, Isaac, and Jacob;[6] that is, he would like to say that there is a unity between Biblical symbolism and the philosophical quest for Being. If such a unity can be maintained, then—to turn a phrase of Hocking's—religions as well as philosophy are fused at the depths. Even if this ultimate unity is elusive (and it should be noted that few philosophers or theologians have followed Tillich in his ultimate synthesis), still in all, his use of the "ground of being" is suggestive of depths in the Christian revelation and of outreach toward an understanding of other religions.

One admission must be made. The identification of the hiddenness of God and the logos *en archē*, which we are implying throughout, might cause some criticism. Particularly is this so when Otto speaks so often of the "non-rational" aspects of religious experience, whereas the logos is bound traditionally with rational explanation—either of the One and the Many, or else of the nature of the Christ. Our only defense against this enigma is a retreat into the mystery of the Godhead. If the hiddenness of God has meaning at all, it is applicable to all persons of the Trinity—particularly to the logos, since the hiddenness is paradoxically tied to the revelation. That the logos is related to the nonrational may be against all Greek precedents, but it is another way of saying that intelligibility is not the sole function of the logos.

1. Rudolf Otto and the Wholly Other

We are going to start with Otto's interpretation of Luther in *The Idea of the Holy*, since we are interested in Otto's relevance for a theological approach to the history of religions.[7] However, it must be admitted at the start that Otto did not treat Luther as the norm for his analysis of the numinous, but only as an example of his own general approach to religion. Otto wanted to put his study on a broad basis, intimately related to the Christian faith, and yet independent enough of the Christian faith so that the study might be related to religion wherever it was found. Strictly speaking, then, Otto belongs to *Religionswissenschaft*, and not to theology—at least in *Das Heilige*. As the very astute scholar Charles A. Bennett says of him, Otto wanted to bring the reader of any religion through a description of the indefinable numinous until the reader exclaimed, "Now I see what you mean." [8]

We would like to consider Otto as a historian of religion, primarily, and see how he describes the example of the nu-

minous in the Christian faith. We will presuppose the kerygma—though Otto does not need to presuppose this to
remain in the field of description. This presupposition is not
difficult to maintain, since Otto so many times seems to be
speaking words in a way that the Christian theologian can
recognize as his own language. In fact, critics have noted
that Otto crosses over into the field of theology many times,
and that this has produced inconsistencies in his writing. For
instance, there is, according to these critics, a tendency for
Otto to confuse the description of the religious consciousness
with the consideration of the object to which it refers. This
confusion brings in an ontology that is separate from the
kerygma and unneeded for his principal work of defending
religious experience as *sui generis*. John Moore rightly observes that a *feeling* of immediate presence can never be the
proof of a real or true presence.[9] Otto constantly describes
the feeling with keen penetration, and states that he has
thereby established the validity of the object associated with
the feeling. This is impossible since there can never be any
cognitive value to feeling. That is why, unlike Otto, we are
assuming the kerygma as a faith commitment, and moving
from the standpoint of theology rather than *Religionswissenschaft*. We will try to benefit from Otto's descriptive
analysis rather than his metaphysical conclusions.

Robert Davidson, who also makes the distinction between
Otto as a phenomenologist and as a theologian, and who interprets him from the phenomenological point of view, quotes
a pertinent observation by H. Höffding in the latter's book,
The Philosophy of Religion: "In any discussion of the significance of religious experience which is to be more than
merely superficial, it will be at any rate helpful—when not
absolutely necessary—to treat the immediately experienced
in as great abstraction as possible from the supposed cause.
That which is strongly and immediately experienced cannot
itself be an illusion. The illusion arises through a false causal
explanation which is confounded with immediate observa-

tion." [10] It is because of his consciousness of this confusion that Davidson undertakes in his study to disentangle Otto's phenomenological analysis of religion from his comment upon its significance and implications. Through Höffding's clarification, the excellence of the descriptive work of Otto's analysis of religion is revealed, free from the limitations and inconsistencies of his comments on its implications. [11]

Another assumption will be made in our study of Otto. We will assume that the religious experience of the kerygma is self-authenticating, much as it seems to be in Luther's theology. This assumption will free Otto's study from another inconsistency, this time in the field of epistemology. In *Das Heilige*, Otto attempted to validate the religious experience through an adaptation of Kant. He tried to posit a unique human capacity for the divination of the numinous, an a priori category, patterned after Kant's categories. [12] Furthermore, Otto adopts Kantian terminology when he speaks of the numinous undergoing schematization. In schematization, the nonrational gives birth to corresponding rational structures. For example, the holy is schematized into the *idea* of the holy. [13] Otto apparently felt that an accurate comprehension of religious knowledge, via Kantian terms, was to be his most important contribution to theology in *Das Heilige*. Actually, this theory of religious knowledge has been subject to all kinds of well-deserved criticism, [14] whereas his historical and psychological interpretation has had wide recognition. [15] It is unfortunate, then, that Otto obscured the fundamental distinction between inner experience and a quasi-Kantian epistemology validating that experience.

By treating the kerygma as the given, and by assuming that it is self-authenticating, we can concentrate on Otto's analysis of the human situation as it is confronted by the kerygma. Thus, we will try to minimize Otto's departure from pure description. Likewise, we shall not be interested in his several "proofs" for the superiority of the Christian faith, which also seem to be a departure from the descriptive role of the historian of religion.

And yet, while we want to see Otto as a historian of religion, with a keen instinct for sensing the effects of the Wholly Other in the religious consciousness, it is particularly suitable that his descriptions be related first of all to the Christian faith before they are related to other faiths. Also, it is fitting that Luther's insights into the nature of God be the focus within Christian theology for what he later was to relate to other theologies. For instance, let us look at an example of "numinous horror," which Otto finds in Luther's sermon on Ex., ch. 20.

Yea, He is more terrible and frightful than the Devil. For, He dealeth with us and bringeth us to ruin with power, smiteth and hammereth us, and payeth no heed to us. . . . In His majesty He is a consuming fire. For therefrom can no man refrain: if he thinketh on God aright, his heart in his body is struck with terror. . . . Yea, as soon as he heareth God named, he is filled with trepidation and fear.

Otto comments on Luther's exposition that it is the absolute numen felt here partially in its aspects of *maiestas* and *tremendum*. Then, in the same context, he goes on to throw some interesting light on the origin of his own approach to the history of religion.

And the reason I introduced these terms above to denote one side of the numinous experience was in fact just because I recalled Luther's own expressions, and borrowed them from his "divina maiestas" and "metuenda voluntas," which have rung in my ears from the time of my earliest study of Luther. Indeed, I grew to understand the numinous and its difference from the rational in Luther's *De Servo Arbitrio* long before I identified it with the "Qadosh" of the Old Testament and in the elements of "religious awe" in the history of religion in general.[16]

On the basis of this testimony, Luther was instrumental in Otto's formulating his descriptive ideas. It is as if, for

Otto, Christian theology were the springboard into *Religions-wissenschaft*. This may account for some of the confusion in the way Otto moves back and forth from phenomenology to Christian theology. For our purposes, we are admitting this confusion in Otto and simply trying to show that it was his Christian experience that opened up his work in the broader field of the history of religions.

Let us grant, then, that he is a historian of religion, but that his descriptive work is an outgrowth of his own Christian religious experience. To recognize this is consistent with Otto's reiterated statement that unless the reader can direct his mind to some deeply felt religious experience there is absolutely no appeal or argument that can be made. (We are not arguing that he ever proves the kerygma from the phenomenological side. Rather, this is accepted by faith, as it was for Luther.) *If* Otto thereupon gives an accurate description of that Christian experience, and *if* (as Otto demonstrates) there are elements in the Christian religious consciousness that have parallels in the religious consciousness of other men, then can some valid revelation be denied to men of these other faiths who possess these similar religious sentiments? It would seem that the Christian's dedication to truth would force some such admission of the validity of other revelations. Such an admission, however, need not be the admission of separate origins of the similar experiences. Quite the reverse. From the theological point of view, the admission is simply that there are depths in the doctrine of God, beyond comprehension but hinted at through *Religionswissenschaft*. In logos terms, there is a "light which lightens every man . . ." The Christian ends by saying that the kerygma has roots that touch more lives than he at first imagined. The God before whom the Christian stands is then not to be localized in Christianity, but is One who has nowhere left himself without witness.

If such an argument will stand up, it would be an interesting case of *Religionswissenschaft*'s asking theology to broaden its base so as to take account of the facts that an exclusivist view of revelation cannot handle. Theology and the history of religions would then be handmaidens. The latter would have the particular function of helping theology to understand its nature. It would force some positive statements about the unknowability of God that would relate to world religions. At the same time it would prevent creedal formulations from becoming the basis of religious intolerance.

2. OTTO'S ANALYSIS OF RELIGIOUS EXPERIENCE

How does Otto analyze the religious experience? We have already been using some of the terms by which he attempts this: "numinous," "Wholly Other," etc. Here, we can do no more than sketch his definitions; particularly since it is his approach that is useful rather than the specific details, or illustrations, that he finds. Otto uses a term to describe any distinctively religious experience. He calls it the "Moment," and believes that this moment is not derived from any other source than itself. It is not a function of evolutionary development, morals, philosophy, and the like. Every religion worthy of the name produces the moment in the worshiper. The content of the moment might be called the "holy" except that this word is associated with moral ideas. More basic, however, than any moral connotation is an overplus of meaning that cannot be strictly defined. It is *sui generis* and irreducible to any other term. The name Otto gives to this overplus of meaning is "numinous." Since the numinous cannot be clearly defined, Otto can only appeal to the reader's "deeply felt religious experience." "Whoever cannot do this, whoever knows no such moments in his experience, is requested to read no further; for it is not easy to discuss questions of religious psychology with one who can recollect the emotions of his adolescence, . . . but cannot recall any intrinsically religious feelings." [17] What the religious experience brings to light is a *creature-consciousness* that is like a shadow cast by that which is an object outside the self.[18]

Creature-consciousness and the numinous are never divorced. Otto feels that creature-consciousness is akin to Schleiermacher's "feeling of dependence." In two ways, however, Schleiermacher is criticized. On the one hand, the "absolute" dependence of Schleiermacher is not *sui generis*. It is only different in degree from "relative" dependence; whereas Otto wants a term designating an intrinsically different quality of experience. On the other hand, Otto criticizes Schleiermacher on the ground that he reaches the "Other" by inference. The absolute dependence is acknowledged first before the object of the feeling is sought. Otto believes that psychologically the numinous and creature-feeling are tied together like object and shadow.

The nature of the numinous is then suggested by means of the special way in which it is reflected in the mind in terms of feeling. In all distinctively religious experiences, there are both *mysterium tremendum* and fascination. Analyzing the first, Otto takes the adjective *tremendum,* and finds it to be made up of three components: awfulness, overpoweringness (*majestas*) and energy or urgency.[19] In discussing each, he finds these elements in the lowest forms of religion as well as in the highest. Particularly does mysticism itself provide a mine of illustrative material. Awe, for instance, may be present among primitives as demonic dread —the feeling of something uncanny, eerie, or weird. Or, it may appear in what Luther refers to as a "shuddering" before God. More than ordinary fear, or even natural fear raised to the highest intensity, is indicated. Actually, it may steal upon the worshiper like a fleeting shadow in his most gentle of moods, or when "Holy, Holy, Holy!" is sung in a hymn.

Overpoweringness (*majestas*) forms "the numinous raw material of religious humility." Otto makes a distinction between "createdness" and "creaturehood." The former is a more innocuous term, stating the fact that we are the work of the divine creative act. Creaturehood, however, "suggests impotence and general nothingness as against overpowering might—dust and ashes as before 'majesty.' In the one case, you have the fact of having been created; in the other, the status of the creature." [20] Such feelings recur constantly as characteristic marks of mysticism in all its forms. The third element of *tremendum* is energy. In the Judeo-Christian tradition, God is the living God. As Luther indicated in his book *The Bondage of the Will*, there is in God a union of majesty with this energy, "in the sense of a force that knows not stint nor stay, which is urgent, active, compelling and alive." [21]

These three characteristics which Otto finds in the *tremendum* are not related analytically to *mysterium;* hence he must also analyze the noun *mysterium*.[22] "Mystery" can mean something that is unexplained at the moment, but that can be explained ultimately. But this is not the sense in which Otto means it. In a religious sense, the mysterious is the Wholly Other—"that which is quite beyond the sphere of the usual, the intelligible and the familiar which therefore falls quite outside the limits of the 'canny' and is contrasted with it, filling the mind with blank wonder and astonishment." [23] It is not because we have come upon the limits of our knowledge that the Wholly Other affects us so. It is rather that the Wholly Other is incommensurable with our knowledge, and therefore "we recoil in a wonder that strikes us chill and numb." [24] It is possible, with the Wholly Other, to use substitute terms like "supernatural" or "transcendent." But these words cannot really put in conceptual terms that which has positive feeling content and which defies the conceptual.

So far, we have been following Otto's analysis of both the adjective and the noun of *mysterium tremendum*. But there is a polarity involved in the numinous experience, something uniquely attractive and fascinating even as it repels.[25] In all genuine religion there is a fascination of the numinous, whereby the worshiper seeks to approach the numen as if his very life depended on it. Paul's words are suggestive of what is meant: "Eye hath not seen, nor ear heard . . . the things which God hath prepared for them that love him" (I Cor. 2:9). Paul's words would parallel those of countless mystics in all religions who point to a blessedness that confounds intellectual expression. Two things about what has been said so far should be kept in mind. One is that these various elements are isolated for purposes of analysis, but not in their true givenness. Analysis is the separation into parts of what really is inseparable. Furthermore, there never exists a pure feeling state which is devoid of creed and cult and all kinds of admixture. Again, analysis is the attempt to see in slow motion the structure of what is always in rapid and kaleidoscopic flux. A second caution should be observed in interpreting Otto. Because he concentrates on unique religious experience that is beyond the rational, this does not mean that the rational is undermined. He says in the foreword to *Das Heilige*:

In this book, I have ventured to write of that which may be called "non-rational" or "supra-rational" in the depths of the divine nature—I do not thereby want to promote in any way the tendency of our time towards an extravagant and fantastic "irrationalism." . . . Before I ventured upon this field of inquiry I spent many years of study upon the rational aspect of that supreme reality we call "God." . . . And I feel that no one ought to concern himself with the *Numen ineffabile* who has not already devoted assiduous and serious study to the *Ratio aeterna*.[26]

More specifically, in the body of the book Otto shows the rational and nonrational in their close relatedness. He says that Christianity, for instance, cannot dispense with the rational; and all talk of the numinous must not blur or diminish its conceptualizing tendencies. But neither can the numinous be disregarded. Simply to rely on the conceptual is to impoverish religion. Actually, the relation of the numinous to the rational could be set up in a logical structure as follows: the numinous, then the ideogram (the symbols or words used to describe it), then the worked-out theology. This order is suggestive because it ties in with a useful suggestion of Peter Munz that in religion, doctrine is always a third removed from the religious experience. Munz does not comment on this numinous experience as he develops his own position, and he is very critical of Otto's metaphysical tendencies.[27] He begins his analysis of religion with symbols, which are more poetic than precise in meaning. It is the symbols that Otto would call ideograms, which are capable of a variety of doctrinal formulations, and hence of a variety of religious branches within any one religion. We have already pointed out how R. L. Slater uses Munz in his attack upon exclusivism in the Christian church. The mere fact that doctrine follows symbol makes for a broadness in interpreting the Christian faith. As Marett once observed, religion is danced out before it is thought out. Otto does not relate the numinous to the doctrinal in such precise detail as Munz, though there are many parallels between the two.

As Otto describes the elements of the numinous, he gives illustrations of his meaning from all religions, present and primitive. A similar search for the numinous is carried on in the New Testament. For instance, the Kingdom of God, interpreted not as a historical goal but as an eschatological "inbreaking," has the marks of genuine religious awe. As such, it colors with mystery all that stands in relation to it. The Lord of this Kingdom, the "heavenly Father," is not any less holy in the New Testament than in the Old Testament. He is the "living God" (Heb. 10:31), the "consuming fire" (Heb. 12:29), the one who dwells in unapproachable light, and so forth. Then, like Luther in *The Bondage of the Will*, Otto finds the doctrine of predestination particularly suggestive of the numinous. There is no explaining it or probing it. It is "nothing but the intensified 'creative feeling' in conceptual expressions, and to be altogether rooted in the numinous consciousness." [28] Finally, Otto finds the moment of religious consciousness not only in the teaching of the New Testament but especially in the person of Christ and in the events of the cross. It was the experience of the holy in Christ that brought men to repentance and to salvation. "The disciples felt, but not as a result of logical compulsion, that if there is a God and if He chose to reveal Himself, he could do it no otherwise than thus."

Because the New Testament abounds in the numinous, Otto was convinced that his stress on personal experience removed the need to defend the Christian faith, as if it could be the victim of a critic's attack. Religious intuitions are "equally unaffected by the fluctuating results of Biblical exegesis and the labored justification of historical apologetics . . . springing as they do from first hand personal divination." [29] In some ways, this conclusion of Otto is the opposite pole from Barth and seems to open Otto to the criticism that Barth and others make, of his having merely a psychology of religion. However, Barth and Otto need not be antagonists. Barth would insist, like Otto, on the Christian faith's being above "the fluctuating results of Biblical exegesis." It is because, for Barth, the word is spoken to us, irrespective of our human criticisms. Yet there is nothing in Otto that forbids there being a theology of the Word. In fact, Otto's answer to Bultmann's problem, "Is Jesus Christ the Son of God because he helps me, or does he help me because he is the Son of God?" might be the reminder that this is not an either/or. As a historian of religion, Otto keeps the former part of the question in view; whereas a theologian might stress the latter. In any event, Barth's criticism of Otto is not entirely fair. For, if it takes two to make a revelation, then there must be some concrete and meaningful criterion in terms of which the transcendent presence and Word of God are distinguished in human experience.[30]

3. THE SIGNIFICANCE OF OTTO FOR A THEOLOGY OF OPENNESS

The value of Otto is at least twofold. From the standpoint of the Christian faith, in his treatment of the numinous and his wealth of illustration from the Bible and Christian history, he gives a great depth to the meaning of God and revelation. The "depth" interpretation seems to go back to his early understanding of Luther's *Deus absconditus,* which he has developed in a much more elaborate fashion. A second value in Otto's approach occurs when we move outside the Christian faith, and allow Otto to be the historian of religion on a wider scale. The experience produced by the Christian revelation has structural similarities in all religions. In every religion there are those "moments" in which the polarity of *mysterium tremendum* and fascination are to be found. In every religion there is creature-feeling, and so forth. Otto's two books on India's religions have ample material showing this is so. For instance, from some points of view Nirvana appears as a cold and negative state, since conceptually it is a negation. Yet, it is felt in the consciousness of the Buddhist as in the strongest degree positive; it exercises a fascination by which its votaries are as much carried away as are the Hindu or the Christian by the corresponding objects of their worship. What is implied here is not a claim that all religions are basically the same, or that there are many equally good roads up the mountain. No one has gone to more exacting scholarship than Otto in showing the differences between mysticism in the East and West, or between "grace" in Bhakti and Christianity. To say, then, that the numinous or the logos is in all religion is not to recommend a reduction of particular religions to one world religion.

For all this, the question is raised whether religious experience might not be as fruitful an area to investigate, when faith meets faith, as doctrine. By the very nature of the numinous, there may not be a way of formulating a statement that religions are "fused at the depth," but there is the undeniable fact that when faithful adherents of two religions meet, "the deep calls unto the deep." There is the further question, which must be left as a question, as to why this is so. As we put it earlier, *if* Otto has accurately described the Christian religious consciousness, and *if* this description fits that of the adherents of other faiths, what is suggested as to the cause? The Christian is theologically committed to Jesus Christ, and for him there is "no other name." Yet we have seen that that is not a simple statement. The logos doctrine, which was discussed in the last chapter, will not allow that particular faith commitment to remain on a propositional level. Through Otto, we have come to the same point, but by a little different route. The question is, Are numinous feelings, genuine in other religions, genuinely produced? Furthermore, do similarities in description indicate similarities in cause? Is there a root in the *Deus absconditus*, which we can neither point out clearly nor deny, that touches the revelation in other faiths? If this were so, and we are outside the realm of the provable, there is no injury done to our own vigorous commitment to Jesus Christ. For one reason, there is only "one way" by which any man worships, namely, through *a* particular faith. As Dean Inge put it, there is no point in being an honorary member of all religions. But more than that, any relation between religions in the hiddenness of God is more a tribute to the majesty of God than a detraction from it. It is a modern awareness of what it must have meant to Isaiah to find that Yahweh was not only the God of the Jews but a light to lighten the Gentiles. For Isaiah, the awareness of a great God was becoming even greater.

4. OTHER THEOLOGIANS OF RELIGIOUS EXPERIENCE

Before we go on to Paul Tillich, we should note that Otto is not alone in stressing the experience of the holy and then relating it to the encounter of world religions. One of the attempts to do so was made by the Scottish theologian John Wood Oman (1860–1939), who carried on his researches quite independently of Otto and yet ended up surprisingly close. Oman analyzed our experience into four elements as it confronts any environment: (*a*) the unique character of the feeling it creates; (*b*) the unique value it has for us; (*c*) the immediate conviction of a special kind of objective reality, which is inseparable from this valuation; and (*d*) the necessity of thinking of it in relation to the rest of experience and the rest of experience in relation to it.[31] This is a formal scheme which he applied to the concrete case of religious experience. Here the unique feeling is the sense of the holy, which is inseparable from a value judgment that the experience is one of incomparable worth—a judgment of the sacred. The sacred, in turn, is not an ethereal sentiment, but attaches to an objective reality in the environment—the supernatural. The supernatural, which is the legitimate sphere of religion, is not that which stands "above" or "beyond" or "underneath" the natural. The natural and the supernatural are given together, "so constantly interwoven that nothing may be wholly natural or wholly supernatural." [32] The fourth element—the relation of the religious experience to the rest of experience—is the realm of theology. As in Otto, the rational follows the experience, and not vice versa.

Oman was not the historian of religion that Otto was, though he used his insight into the nature of the supernatural to classify various religious types. Thus, where the supernatural is conceived as a vague force diffused through the natural, there is *primitive animism*. The attempt to manage the natural through faith in individual supernatural

spirits believed to rule over the various parts of the natural
is *polytheism*. *Mysticism* is associated with the pantheistic
acceptance of the natural in its wholeness as the supernatural. *Legalistic* religion is associated with a dualism that
sharply distinguishes the sacred from the profane. Last of
all, there is *prophetic* religion and true monotheism. With
the prophetic type there is the "reconciliation to the natural
by faith in one personal Supernatural who gives meaning to
the natural and has a purpose beyond it." [33] In all of this
analysis, Oman was more the philosopher than either theologian or historian of religion.

Another theologian who made much of religious experience is Herbert H. Farmer, who gave the Gifford Lectures
of 1950. The title of Farmer's book is *Revelation and Religion*, though the subtitle is more revealing—"Studies in the
Theological Interpretation of Religious Types." [34] In the
Preface, Farmer indicates his great indebtedness to John
Oman, and in the body of the book there are several tributes
to Rudolf Otto. The difference from both men is that Farmer
is an avowed theologian who would like to develop a world
view—one that includes the world religions—from the Christian faith. He feels that enough phenomenologies of religion
have been written; as well as enough theologies that do not
take any interest in the general religious life of man. For
himself, he makes no apologies for a theology that is within
the limits of traditional orthodoxy. However, there are two
facts that keep this dogma from tending toward an exclusivist point of view. One of these is that he is willing to hold
on to his dogma as a hypothesis to be proved rather than as
a conclusion to be believed. As he puts it, a Christian doctrine should never be introduced in an *ad hoc* and over-
riding way, no matter how deeply convinced of that doctrine
the thinker himself may be. In this willingness to expose
doctrine to the wide ranges of thought and knowledge in
other religions, Farmer is engaging in what Kenneth Cragg
has termed "frontier theology." A second factor which

keeps Farmer's dogma flexible is that he senses that underneath theology there must be a vital life of religious experience. In this, the teachings of Otto and Oman play their part. To attempt a purely detached and objective study, says Farmer, is an *ignis fatuus*. Or, quoting the more picturesque words of Oman, "If we do not know already what religion is, we can no more hope to reconstruct a living religion out of a welter of facts than if we had never seen a tree to reconstruct it out of sawdust." [35]

It is Farmer's attempt to get under the Christian dogma, as it were, and sense a vital element in that dogma—and in all religion—that is his justification for lecturing under the Gifford Trust, which stated that only natural theology should be treated. There is, for Farmer, a subjective element inalienable from all theological statement. Underneath all intellectual and reflective processes involved in any religion there is an "inward disposition" that has deep roots in the personality. Christian theism is no exception here. If Christian theism is compelling, it is not because it has succeeded in winning a battle in logic. Rather, it is because it has penetrated to and evoked a sense of truth that lies deeper than logic and comprehends more of the whole man as a willing and feeling as well as a thinking being. This being so, Farmer feels that if the Christian experience can be analyzed in its depths, then some contact can be made with other religions that also are "living religions" only insofar as this depth is at the root of their varied expressions. It is because of Farmer's attempt to take the dogmatic and see that it rests upon nonrational facts that we classify him in the same category as Otto and Oman.

In analyzing the distinctively Christian experience, Farmer asks what is involved in the Christian act of worship. By this he hopes to get to the "inward *Tiefe*," which cannot be discerned by bringing a detached analytical mind to bear on the outward manifestations of the Christian faith. If he can find what is involved in the act of Christian worship, the result will be not only greater self-understanding of the Christian faith, but a normative concept whereby he can begin to classify other religions. In this, the influence of his teacher, John Oman, is most apparent.

We will not follow in any detail his elaborate analysis of Christian worship. He does so by using the formula "God— Father, Son, and Holy Spirit," taking each term in turn but bearing in mind all the time that in so doing he is splitting up for purposes of exposition that which is a unitary apprehension and act. Of particular interest in Farmer's discussion is his treatment of the Holy Spirit. J. Wach said in many of his writings that the doctrine of the Holy Spirit held much promise for guiding the future encounter of the Christian faith and other faiths. It is by taking seriously the Holy Spirit in worship that Farmer gets beyond such time-tested pairs of words as transcendence/immanence or personal/ impersonal. God is not only (so to say) merely "out there." He is also "a mysterious, sustaining, creative and recreative power within, having access to and being at work within those *dunkle Tiefe* of the soul of which the worshipper himself is only dimly conscious, if conscious at all." [36] Saying this, Farmer goes on to a very suggestive idea, familiar in Paul Tillich and Carl Jung, that the conception of God as personal can be stated in such a way as to lose sight of the mysterious depths of the unconscious. When that occurs, the result is what Jung terms an "unbearably refined 'I-Thou' relationship to God." [37] Here Farmer finds that Otto's analysis of mysticism is extremely helpful. In Otto's book *Mysticism East and West,* the point is made that mysticism always conceived God otherwise than in relations between "I and Thou." Farmer allows Otto to speak for him.

[Transcendence and immanence] is "not only too colorless and cold, but is inadequate to give the true and living content of this antinomy. The antithesis is rather this: that the divine, which on the one hand is conceived in symbols taken from the personal sphere as Lord, King, Father, Judge—a person in relation to persons—is on the other hand also denoted in dynamic symbols as the power of life, as light and life, as spirit ebbing and flowing . . . , a glowing fire that penetrates and pervades. It is characterized as the principle of a renewed, supernatural Life, mediating and giving itself, breaking forth in the living man . . . as an inward principle of the power of new being and life. Without this mystery, Christianity were no Christianity. But with it, 'simple' Christianity . . . knows Godhead, not at this point conceived in any relationship of I-Thou, but as a permeating principle of light and life, not to be addressed, but to be experienced." [38]

We have quoted this passage at some length, not only to show Farmer's indebtedness to Rudolf Otto but also to indicate the very suggestive way in which Farmer moves from orthodox formulation to incisive observations concerning the Christian experience. And the experience that is brought to light swings back to enlighten the nature of God, which has given birth to the experience.

Farmer's discussion of the Holy Spirit, which concludes his attempt to discover the essence of Christian worship through the analysis of the triune name of God, leads to a tabulation of his findings. Before giving these, Farmer feels the necessity of referring to another element in worship. It concerns *the element of feeling that pervades the whole encounter with God in worship*. Here again, the influence of Otto is seen.

We may not be able to accept his [Otto's] treatment of the matter in all its detail . . . but his basic insistence on the *sui generis* quality of the feeling element in the living apprehension of God, corresponding to the uniqueness of the divine reality thus apprehended (which uniqueness he indicated by coining the distinctive term "numinous"), is certainly right. Numinous feeling, if we care to use the phrase, is the distinctive feeling-tone which reverberates through the whole being when God is livingly encountered and only when He is livingly encountered.[39]

It is very disappointing that in Farmer's classification of religions, this element of the numinous does not play any part at all. Yet it is important to see the place he gives to it as a theologian, which is comparable to the place Otto gives to it as a phenomenologist.

Farmer's discussion of worship concludes with seven findings, which he realizes are the "barest bones of abstract statement." [40] The seven, which will become the basis of classifying other religions, are as follows: (a) the apprehension of God as the *ontologically other;* that is to say, as the ultimate source of all being, the one self-subsistent underived Reality from which all else, including the worshiper himself, draws a wholly dependent existence; (b) the apprehension of God as the *axiologically other,* as being in himself the realized perfection of all value; (c) the apprehension of God as *personal;* (d) the apprehension of God as *asking all;* (e) the apprehension of God as *giving all,* even while claiming all; (f) the apprehension of the personal God as *intimately present and active* within the worshiper's own being, the inward source of life and power; and (g) a *feeling tone,* pervading the whole awareness, which is akin to awe, but which is really *sui generis* and can only be described as the feeling tone that accompanies and is appropriate to the living encounter with God.

This feeling tone, as we said above, does not figure at all when the other elements become normative. If it were developed along with the others, perhaps the nearness of the relation between the religions would be more in evidence, as it is, for instance, when Otto discusses India's religions. However, Farmer does feel that "*all* the elements which the analysis of Christian worship has revealed will *tend* to be present together in however obscure, faint, or fleeting, or germinal or perverted a form." Christianity, however, remains normative for him and all other religions fall short in the way they omit certain of the remaining six criteria.

Farmer is open to many criticisms of his approach, of course. Kraemer chides him that in his desire to see other religions in a positive way he has a "too great subservience to

the desire—in itself excellent—to be fair." [41] Macquarrie
rightly criticizes Farmer that in making Christianity normative in such an absolute way, he runs the risk of distorting
other religions.[42] The religions that Farmer discusses hardly
appear to be the living religions that claim the faith of millions of adherents. In fairness to Farmer, however, it must
be admitted that the theologian always appears to distort
by the very nature of the faith commitment that is involved
in theology. That is why theology can never be an isolated
discipline in the field of world religions. Theology, if it is to
work on the "frontiers," must be informed and balanced by
phenomenology. Admitting this, however, we can hope to
delineate only the type of theology that can best provide
for the encounter of living religions. This type, as we have
tried to show from Otto, Oman, and Farmer, is such that
will attempt to say something positive about the mystery
of God, which strangely enough is saying something about
the unique emotions of the human personality, which are
found universally.

CHAPTER
V

The Logos
and Radical Continuity

In many ways, Tillich—who speaks so much of symbolism
—is a symbol himself of the need to be open to other religions because of the very nature of the Christian's theological
commitment. He is a logos theologian and has ties to Rudolf
Otto and theologians of religious experience. Needless to
say, he is at the opposite extreme from Hendrik Kraemer.
If Kraemer speaks for radical discontinuity, Tillich speaks
for theological openness, or radical continuity. Whether or
not he can be followed by the Christian church in his statement of the logos will be the crucial question. If the logos
becomes, in Tillich's hands, a principle of intelligibility more
than the logos who meets us decisively in the historic figure
of Jesus Christ, then the limits of openness have been
reached. In that case, some restatement of the logos as a
theological norm will have to be made. However, before
criticizing Tillich, we must follow his analysis.

In the last lecture he gave before his death, entitled "The
Significance of the History of Religions for the Systematic
Theologian," he summarized his general position by disavowing two extreme ways of looking at world religions from the
standpoint of Christian theology. One is Barthian exclusivism, which rejects out of hand all religions other than the
religion of the theologian. The other is a theology of the
secular. Both extremes, interestingly enough, have this in
common, that they can be reduced to the figure of Jesus. The
Barthians do it by making Jesus of Nazareth the exclusive

place where revelation can be heard. The secular theologians do it by making Jesus of Nazareth the representative of a theologically relevant secularity. Against both groups, Tillich urges a series of presuppositions, some of which have been incorporated already in this thesis:[1]

1. Revelatory experiences are universally human. Something that makes religions possible is given to man where he lives. Furthermore, a revelation once given implies saving powers.
2. Revelation is received by man in terms of his finite human situation and, therefore, in a distorted form.
3. A theologian assumes not only particular revelatory experiences, but a criterion whereby to criticize these experiences.
4. A theologian assumes the possibility of a central event in the history of religions that unites the interpretation of all revelatory experiences and that makes possible "a concrete theology with universal significance."
5. The history of religions does not lie in a realm alongside the history of culture. Rather, the sacred is the creative ground as well as the critical judgment of the secular.

Unless the theologian accepts these five presuppositions, Tillich does not feel he can affirm any serious significance of the history of religions for theology. Presupposition 5 is especially aimed against the secular theologians, while 1 and 2 have particular pointedness against exclusivism.

1. THE ONTOLOGICAL APPROACH TO GOD

It is difficult to point out Tillich's method of approaching other religions without becoming involved in a discussion of his entire system. The latter is quite beyond the scope of our interest. It should be noted, however, that from the time of his trip to Japan in 1960, and subsequent to his involvement with Mircea Eliade, Tillich was in the process of rethinking his entire systematic theology from the standpoint of the history of religions. As he puts it: "In these seminars [with Eliade] I experienced that every individual doctrinal statement or ritual expression of Christianity receives a new intensity of meaning and a kind of apologia, yet also a self-accusation. I must say that my own *Systematic Theology* was written before these seminars and had another intention; namely, the apologetic discussion against and with the secular. . . . But perhaps we need a longer, more intensive period of interpretation, of systematic theological study and religious historical studies." Such a need to see theology in the broadest context is commendable, but there are certain limitations. One is that the attempt to be open to truth from all sources and to reinterpret Christian truth in the light of that new truth can involve the theologian in making his own theology too ambiguous. When all is said and done, a critic must ask Tillich if he still is speaking about a Christian faith that would be acceptable to the theologians of that faith. Another limitation is that Tillich's attempt to include the history of religions in a schema in the same way that he has absorbed philosophy and culture, gives the appearance of his attempting an ultimate synthesis that is impossible to the human mind. A philosopher or a historian could criticize Tillich's position in that it does not allow him the freedom to develop his own discipline.[2] By far the more serious criticism is the former. If what Tillich has in the end is a theology which does not represent that of the church at large, then his encounter is weakened. That is, he can meet, from the standpoint of his own unique Christian theology, adherents of other religions (with valuable insights accruing therefrom), but he cannot describe this meeting as one between Christianity and the world religions.

Despite the fact that Tillich felt that his mind had changed in his last six years, everything in his last lecture on the history of religions can be found somewhere in Volume I of the *Systematic Theology,* particularly in the sections on

"Being and God." What is proposed here is to give a brief statement of his approach to the doctrine of God, since this is always the basis for his encounter with world religions. Then we shall see how his understanding of that doctrine led him into a deep appreciation of Eastern religions, particularly Buddhism. Following this we shall offer a few criticisms. Such criticisms are not meant to cancel the appreciations of Tillich's broad point of view, but to indicate limitations in the finely honed system. What will be apparent is that from this writer's point of view, Paul Tillich is most convincing when he speaks of religious experience and when he points to the depths of God. He is least convincing when he attempts the ultimate synthesis of philosophy (or history of religions, etc.) and theology. The parallel between Rudolf Otto and Tillich is noticeable, since Otto also is more convincing in describing the personal experience of the holy than in his metaphysical deductions.

One of the most illuminating essays of Tillich, which sets the stage for his later broad inclusivism, is "The Two Types of Philosophy." [3] In his essay, Tillich contrasts an Aristotelian approach to God, which he calls cosmological, with an Augustinian approach, which he calls ontological. In the first, God is met accidentally as a result of inference. Essentially, according to Thomas, God and man do not belong to each other, and the line is sharply drawn between the natural and the supernatural. God is a stranger who is known unconditionally only by himself. Man, on the other hand, being excluded from the *primum esse*, knows God only by his effects (hence the term "cosmological" approach, since it rests on causality). As a result of man's limited knowledge, there is a basic split, which Tillich protests, between faith and knowledge, between God and Being, between theology and philosophy. If Being becomes *a* Being (God), then a barrier is set up between the ultimate of the Being and all other ultimates.

The second way of approaching God is the ontological

path, which Tillich attributes to Augustine. Here the estrangement between God and man is overcome, since man discovers himself when he discovers God. He discovers something identical with himself although it transcends him infinitely, something from which he is estranged, but from which he has never been separated. God in the ontological approach is identical with Being, or with truth itself. He is not the conclusion reached after a series of inferences, nor is he the object of a question. Quite the reverse. God is the presupposition of the question of God. Rather than being the most powerful being, God is the power of being. He is the "identity of subject and object, the principle of knowledge, the first truth in light of which everything else is known." All the separate cleavages mentioned in the cosmological approach are broken down. Faith becomes a form of knowledge, God and Being (not *a* Being) are one, theology and philosophy have the same Ultimate Reality. It is easy to see how such an all-inclusive principle can ultimately handle world religions in the same way as it handles all other areas of thought and cultures.

Just as Kraemer, Perry, Frick, and the Barthian school judge all religions other than the Christian faith to be merely the result of human striving, Tillich, on the other hand, finds the members of all faiths dealing with the same ultimate concern. In fact, after his visit to Japan, he reported that he was impressed by the ultimate concern he found in forms of religious life uninfluenced by Christianity. He says that his observations there strengthened his theological conviction that the concept of religion in its larger sense "transcends the concrete existence of any religion, as God transcends each of his manifestations." [4] Such a testimonial seems to be a logical outgrowth of his ontological approach to God. There is another insight that grows out of the ontological approach, and this is worthy of comment, since it is a continual source of ambiguity in *The Idea of the Holy*. When Rudolf Otto discussed "the holy" from a phenomenological point of view, the analysis was weakened by an intrusion of metaphysics. The question could always be asked of Otto as to how he could speak of *tremendum* and fascination as being produced in the worshiper and assume that these were correlated to a Wholly Other. For Tillich, this particular ambiguity disappears. Instead of speaking of God as *a* Being who is "Wholly Other," he uses more suggestive concepts of "being-itself" or "ground of being." The use of these concepts means that any phenomenological description of the experience of religion in man has to be at the same time a description of the nature of God.

Very much related to the identity (and transcendence) of the subject-object structure of reality is Tillich's discussion of the two concepts of reason.[5] There is technical reason, which is man's capacity for reasoning. Technical reason deals with means rather than ends. It systematizes, criticizes, investigates, and so forth, but without ever raising the existential questions, What is the meaning of life? and What is my ultimate concern? But Tillich believes reason has a logos structure also, which he calls the "ontological concept of reason," and which is correlated to the logos structure of the universe. Ontological reason is the noncognitive side of reason, whereby man is involved in existential concerns, and whereby he can "grasp and shape" the world about him. This identity of the logos structure of the mind and universe is quite foreign to the spirit of modern philosophy, despite the long line of philosophers from Parmenides to Hegel who developed a similar approach. Perhaps it will appeal or not depending on whether the reader has felt the distinction between inner direction and manipulation from without, between making the wheels of society turn and sensing the direction the wheels should move. However, leaving criticism aside for the moment, such an identity of thought and being allows Tillich to develop a point of view that has far-reaching implications for interfaith dialogue. As he states at the beginning of the *Systematic Theology:*

Christianity does not need a "Christian philosophy" in the narrower sense of the word. The Christian claim that the *logos* who has become concrete in Jesus as the Christ is at the same time the universal *logos* includes the claim that wherever the *logos* is at work it agrees with the Christian message. No philosophy which is obedient to the universal *logos* can contradict the concrete *logos,* the Logos "who became flesh." [6]

We have not yet indicated the place of Jesus Christ in Tillich's scheme. But it is obvious that the sentence "No philosophy which is obedient to the universal *logos* can contradict the concrete *logos*" might also read "No world religion which . . . " Certainly the religions of the world participate in the same *logos* structure that Tillich finds in the human psyche. In fact, Tillich says this explicitly in his later article, "How My Mind Has Changed."

Eastern wisdom, like every other wisdom, certainly belongs to the self-manifestations of the logos, and must be included in the interpretation of Jesus as the Christ if he is rightly to be called the incarnation of the logos.[7]

We must come back to this statement later. Meanwhile, there is a second way in which the ontological concept of reason, what Tillich calls "the depth of reason," has significance for the encounter of world religions. He says: "The depth of reason is the expression of something which is not reason but which precedes reason and is manifest through it. Reason in both its objective and subjective structures points to something which appears in these structures but which transcends them in power and meaning." Tillich calls it "being-itself," though it can only be another term for God. In a very significant sentence, Tillich says that "the statement that God is being-itself is a nonsymbolic statement. It does not point beyond itself. It means what it says directly and properly. . . . However, after this has been said, nothing else can be said about God as God which is not symbolic." [8] If this is to be taken at its face value, it means that the depth of reason is the depth of every man in whatever faith he happens to be—and the "depth" can be called either "God" or "being-itself." This leads to the question of the importance (or nonimportance) of Jesus Christ. If all men have God in the depths, what is the need for "God in Jesus Christ"? The answer to this question will involve Tillich's concept of the New Being, his concept of the tension between universality and particularity, and his doctrine of dynamic typology. Let us consider these in connection with his view of the encounter between religions.

2. TILLICH'S VIEW OF THE ENCOUNTER OF WORLD RELIGIONS

The encounter that Tillich envisages between religions can be seen from the standpoint of two basic concepts. One is what he calls "the inescapable inner tension in the idea of God," the tension between concreteness and the ultimacy, or universality, of the religious concern. This first concept has some of the characteristics of Hocking's description of the universal and particular in religion. However, Tillich can use this tension in more sophisticated ways. By it he can characterize the attitude of the Christian faith to other religions (Ch. 2 of *Christianity and the Encounter of the World Religions*); he can classify religions and their philosophical equivalents (Sec. II, 2, of "Being and God," *Systematic Theology,* Vol. I); he can set forth the principle whereby Christianity judges itself (Ch. 4 of *Christianity and the Encounter of the World Religions*); and finally, he can give his interpretation of the incarnation in relation to the encounter. The second basic concept is not put to multiple use, as is the first, but it is important for the flexibility of the interfaith dialogue. This is Tillich's term, "dynamic typology," with its corollary of the *telos* of each religion.

Before we look more closely at these two basic concepts, a preliminary observation is in order. This concerns the broad way Tillich treats the subject of religion. If religion is defined in the usual sense by reference to the term "God," or "gods," then Zen Buddhism could not qualify as a religion, nor could secular movements that have a religious fervor. For Tillich, religion is: "the state of being grasped by an ultimate concern, a concern which qualifies all other concerns as preliminary and which itself contains the answer to the question of the meaning of our life." [9] With this definition, Tillich can include Communism, Fascism, National Socialism, Liberal Humanism, etc., as quasi religions, in that they rest on an ultimate concern just as the other world religions do. This is a much more precise approach than that of Toynbee, who wants to include these ideologies also and have the great religions work together to combat the dangers in them. But he lacks the concept that defines them as religious movements. As a result, Toynbee cannot adequately describe the dynamic element in the encounter, both the inner threat and positive contribution, of these quasi religions. Tillich can, and does; and while we are not going to deal with Chapter 1 of *Christianity and the Encounter of the World Religions,* he has many acute observations on what has been happening in different parts of the world as the quasi religions have been interacting with world religions proper.

But let us return to the first of our two basic concepts— the tension between the concrete expression of religious concern (in myth, cult, incarnation, dogma, etc.) and the ultimacy of that concern. Tillich defines the spheres in which this tension operates. There is the divine sphere, which uses a phenomenological description of the meaning of God. Every religion, including Christianity, attempts such a description. God or gods are the symbols of man's ultimate concern. If God is understood in this way, early Buddhism has a concept of God just as certainly as does Vedanta Hinduism. By stressing the divine sphere, the meaning of God, Tillich hopes he can avoid the danger inherent in both Schleiermacher and Rudolf Otto, of transforming religion into an aesthetic-emotional experience. In addition to the divine sphere, there is the corresponding sphere of holiness. Whenever the divine (God) is manifest, a sacred realm is established which can be described as the holy and which is the most adequate basis we have for understanding the divine. The tension between concrete and ultimate operates in the spheres of both the divine and the holy. For instance, while the divine demands "absolute intensity, infinite passion," there must be some concrete expression in myth and cult or in ethical action. Here is the possibility of the tension breaking down, and of gods becoming objects and tools. Similarly, while the holy must become actual through holy "objects," here again, there is the danger of such objects being thought holy in and of themselves, rather than through their relation to the divine. In this case, where the holy objects do not "negate themselves" and point to the divine of which they are objects, an idol is formed. Objects and their ground are always in delicate balance.

On the basis of this tension which operates in the spheres of the divine and of the holy, Tillich proceeds to group the types of religion. "The concreteness of man's ultimate concern drives him toward polytheistic structures; the reaction of the absolute element against these drives him toward monotheistic structures; and the need for a balance between the concrete and the absolute drives him toward trinitarian structures." [10] This sentence we will allow to stand for the intricate descriptions of "types of polytheism" and "types of monotheism," both of which are preparations for final revelation in the Christian faith. As a schema, Tillich's analysis has some value. However, on the whole it seems an artificial arrangement, too much influenced by Hegel, which does not do justice to world religions as the faiths of real men. Also it seems to prearrange the elements in world religions so that Trinitarian monotheism shows up too easily as the apex of a triangle of which "types of polytheism" and "types of monotheism" are the base points. Such a method of using the tension in the idea of God to classify the world religions is held to, even in the last period of Tillich's life when he has met Buddhism firsthand.

There is another way in which the tension between the concrete and the ultimate figures, and this is in Tillich's description and use of the incarnation.

These quotations will set the argument for what follows:

a. It is necessary [for the Christian theologian] to accept the vision of early Christianity that if Jesus is called the Christ he must represent everything particular and *must be the point of identity between the absolutely concrete and the absolutely universal.*[11]

b. The first and basic answer theology must give to the question of the finality of the revelation in Jesus as the Christ is the following: a revelation is final if it has the power of negating itself without losing itself. . . . Jesus of Nazareth is the medium of final revelation because he sacrifices himself completely to Jesus as the Christ.[12]

c. Jesus is the religious and theological object as the Christ and only as the Christ. And he is the Christ as the one who sacrifices what is merely "Jesus" in him. The decisive trait in his picture is the continuous self-surrender of Jesus who is Jesus to Jesus who is the Christ.[13]

In Jesus as the Christ, Tillich finds the perfect balance between concrete and ultimate. But there is more. In Jesus as the Christ there is a principle that sets the attitude of the Christian to other faiths. Tillich calls this attitude "conditional exclusivism." [14] It is the acceptance of Jesus as the Christ, and yet, paradoxically, the rejection of a particularism that would turn the Christian faith into a form of idolatry. Or, from a slightly different point of view, conditional exclusivism is the acceptance of everything in other faiths that points back to the divine (as Jesus the Christ points back to the divine); and it is the rejection of everything that turns the sacred into a finite object. Acceptance and rejection

are terms derived from the tension between the concrete and
the universal,[15] and these in turn rest on the perfect tension
in the incarnation itself. This means that the encounter with
other religions, or quasi religions, will always have a dialectical appearance. There will never be a total rejection of
another faith, no more than there can be a total acceptance.

Tillich believes that the history of Christianity will show
that his dialectical approach has been conspicuous in most
centuries. This contradicts the popular assumption that
Christianity had an exclusively negative attitude toward
other faiths. The Fathers of the early centuries, for instance,
never treated other religions as totally wrong. Following the
idea of the logos, they could say with Augustine that the true
religion had always existed among the ancients and was
called Christianity only after the appearance of Christ.[16]
Tillich believes that this early Christian attitude of accept-
ance/rejection should be the guide for the present encounter.
Such an openness to other faiths has not been a consistent
testimony of Christian history, however. The seventh-cen-
tury Muslim movement, with its warlike approach to the
West, produced an understandable narrowing of the Christian outlook into a fanatical exclusiveness. The Crusades
were the climax of this fanaticism and a radical attitude
took hold on an even broader scale, as witnessed in anti-
Semitism. However, in all eras of church history, men such
as Nicholas of Cusa, Erasmus, and Zwingli carried on the
early universalism of the Fathers and maintained the tension between the absolutely concrete and absolutely universal. It was Tillich's hope that this type of thought will pre-
vail in modern times.

This leads to a final way in which Tillich uses the tension
between the particular and universal, namely, Christianity's
self-judgment. If, in Christianity's central event, the particular in Jesus Christ has been crucified for the sake of the
universal, then Christianity can proceed to judge all its
particular expressions. Nothing particular dares become an

idol. The Bible fights for God against the concreteness of religion, says Tillich. Jesus violated the ritual law in order to exercise love. Paul did the same for the sake of freedom in Christ. Luther attacked the monastic forms in order to defend the sanctity of the secular realm. The list of examples could be extended indefinitely. Tillich feels that his own idea of the "God above God" is another such example. It is an attempt to break down the belief in *one* God who is bound to a particular group, in favor of a meaning which is not to be circumscribed by any particularity.

What all this means for world religions is that there should be no attempt to "convert" in the usual sense of the word. To convert would mean that the dogmas, organizations, etc., of the Christian faith were above serious criticism and were the only concrete means whereby man could express his ultimate concern. Instead of attempts at converting others, there should be a dialogue in which all participants would be changed. Yet, for Christianity to be in dialogue, accepting criticism and provoking it, does not mean the giving up of its traditions and dogmas. Particularity must remain, but particularity must be broken through. The result is an openness to every other religion. Tillich says:

In the depth of every living religion there is a point at which the religion itself loses its importance, and that to which it points breaks through its particularity, elevating it to spiritual freedom and with it to a vision of the spiritual presence in other expressions of the ultimate meaning of man's existence.

This is what Christianity must see in the present encounter of world religions.[17]

So far we have been looking at the variety of ways in which Tillich uses the tension in the idea of God, a tension between concrete expression and universal or ultimate significance. It figures in the way he classifies religions, in the way he sees the Christian faith judging non-Christian religions, in the way he interprets the incarnation, and in the way the Christian faith is self-critical. There is one final term that is important in Tillich's "encounter" with world religion, and this is "dynamic typology." Types never exist in concrete cases. Types are ideal structures that are approximated by concrete things or events without every being attained. Nothing historical completely represents a particular type, but everything historical is nearer to or farther away from a particular type. Ordinarily, types are thought to be static and unrelated. Tillich, on the other hand, in speaking about types of religion, finds that these ideals have polar tensions in them that make them in the process of change. They are dynamic. There are elements in each type that conflict and that change the relation of the types to one another in different generations. These conflicting elements in any one religion not only make for change, but they also provide the possibility of dialogue between religions. The only reason that a Hindu and a Muslim can converse profitably is that while each is in a different type of religion, each has points in common with the other. Such points are not only tensions within the religions themselves but silent bonds between them.

As an illustration of this, Tillich described his dialogue with Buddhist monks. Christianity and Buddhism have not had much contact with each other historically. And, from many points of view, they seem to be antagonistic. Christianity's experience of the holy has emphasized the ethical. What drives it along (its *telos*) is that it sees "every*one* and everything united in the Kingdom of God." Buddhism's experience of the holy is mystical. Its *telos* is to see "every*thing* and everyone fulfilled in the Nirvana." [18] Nirvana is an ontological symbol. Its material is taken from the experience of finitude, separation, blindness, suffering, and it points to the blessed oneness of everything beyond finitude and error in the ultimate ground of being. This leads to great differences, between Christianity and Buddhism, and seemingly impossible barriers. One of these which is of practical moment is the way these two religions relate to the political sphere. Christianity expresses its ultimate concern in personal categories, and this has given a sturdiness to the democracy of the West. Japan is now a democracy, but without the spiritual heritage that makes democracy possible. It does not have the symbol of the Kingdom of God, which gives the impulse for a radical transformation of society.

Yet, though the symbols Kingdom of God and Nirvana are so different, the basis for dialogue cannot be written off. Within each of the two religions Tillich finds that there are other elements than those which predominate. For instance, the mystical element is not lacking in Christianity. On the other hand, in Mahayana Buddhism, the Buddha-Spirit appears in many manifestations of a personal character, making a nonmystical, often very primitive relation to a divine figure possible. All of this shows that the various elements that constitute the meaning of the holy in one religion are never completely lacking in the other. These various elements in one religion produce constant and creative tension. Lutheran mystics, for instance, often come near a kind of nature mysticism that would be abhorrent to Calvinistic Protestantism. But what is tension within any religion is the basis for dialogue between religions. And the elements of the experience of the holy—elements like the mystical and ethical—are always in the process of change when dialogue is going on.

3. An Evaluation of Tillich's Encounter

There are many advantages of Tillich's dynamic typology over other forms of structure. For instance, Hegel's dialectic traced the movement of the World Spirit, but without the possibility of creative interaction. In Hegelian dialectics, Buddhism is considered as an early stage of religious development that was totally abandoned by history. Tillich will not speak of any evolutionary interpretation of the history of religion. Rather, he says: "In the history of religion . . . each gain in one respect is accompanied by a loss in another respect. . . . Therefore, if the theologian speaks of elements of progress in the history of religion, he must refer to those developments in which the contradiction between the ultimate element and the concrete element in the idea of God is fragmentarily overcome."[19] Tillich, of course, is not alone in criticizing the idea of historical progress among religions. Berdyaev does the same thing from a metaphysical standpoint not too different from Tillich. For him, as for Tillich, any perfect historical epoch of the past or the future is an impossibility. The fundamental conclusion of Berdyaev's metaphysics of history is that "there is an urge of history toward superhistory, an urge which has the possibility of fulfillment in the freedom of man."[20] This statement is set in a different context from what we have been considering, but it has the same sound as to say that the concrete must "negate itself," or become "transparent to" the ultimate. The dynamism of history for both men is not historical progress but constant interaction and tension between polar elements.

One other advantage of a dynamic typology is the possibility of doing justice to a wider variety of characteristics in each of the religions. For instance, the difference between Tillich and Schweitzer is most obvious at just this point. Schweitzer, in his two books *Christianity and the Religions of the World*[21] and *Indian Thought and Its Development*,[22] analyzes the differences of East and West in terms of the mystical versus the ethical, somewhat as Tillich does. However, there is no feeling for the tension *within* and the tension *between* the religions.

Schweitzer used three criteria to distinguish religious types. Are they optimistic or pessimistic? A religion that is pessimistic looks only beyond the world. Optimistic religions believe there are forces at work in the natural world that emanate from a primal source. A second criterion is: Are they monistic or dualistic? A religion is dualistic if God is over against the world and unknown and yet at the same time is in us as an ethical ideal. It is monistic if to know the universe is to know God. The third criterion is the extent

to which ethical activity is present. Since Schweitzer has
already described the essence of Christianity as the response
to an ethical will, and since he operates with the conviction
that Christianity is the deepest expression of the religious
mind, then it is obvious that these three criteria will not only
be a means for grouping religions but also for demonstrating
the superiority of the Christian faith. Christianity is dualistic
and highly ethical, and has a productive tension between
optimism and pessimism. This is both its nature and its
superiority. However, the Christianity Schweitzer discusses
is too static and its superiority too easily arrived at. Furthermore, he has no structure for describing how Christianity's
ethical element is played upon from within by forces that
are dominant in Eastern religions. For instance, it will be
remembered that Radhakrishnan quoted extensively from
Hindu literature to show that the latter can have a strong
ethical, world-affirming attitude.[23] And, conversely, he quoted
Christian authors whose lines are as world-negating as any
of Hinduism's.

Yet, despite all of Schweitzer's overstatement, and the
penetrating criticism of Radhakrishnan, there is still evidence that the former has touched on a difference that cannot entirely be cleared up by the latter's apologetic. After
running through all kinds of criticism against Schweitzer,
Radhakrishnan addresses himself to the question whether
Hindu ethics treats inner perfection as of more importance
than ethical activity. He pleads guilty to the charge. "The
motive behind ethical practices is that of purging the soul of
selfish impulses so that it may be fitted to receive the beatific
vision." [24] But that is just the point of difference. Ethics for
the Hindu is a means to something else that will be of benefit to the ethical performer. In Christianity, ethics is a response to a holy God, which response has its rewards, but
which is not made primarily for that personal reward. It is
hard to conceive of Amos, or any of the prophets for that

matter, subscribing to the motive of ethical activity to which Radhakrishnan has pleaded guilty.

This points up the dilemma, then, of having to recognize dominant characteristics that conflict across religious boundaries along with recessive characteristics that may conflict *within* any one religion but have affinity with elements in other religions. For instance, the personal God in Christianity is a dominant element, but never without the recessive "God above God." In Buddhism, Nirvana is dominant, but never without the personal bodhisattva ideal. To see these various polarities and their interaction is the valid aim of Tillich's dynamic typology, and is a welcome construct. The only additional criticism that could be offered is that Tillich could be even more helpful if he knew the other faiths from the inside, as it were. Three months in Japan is hardly enough time to know Buddhism. Rudolf Otto, to whom Tillich seems indebted for many of his phenomenological observations concerning the holy, has a broader knowledge obviously lacking in Tillich. A combination of Otto's knowledge of world religions and Tillich's existential analysis would give the basis for a solid theological advance in the late twentieth century.

One criticism of Tillich we have saved until the last, and that concerns his Christology. Whether Tillich can lead the bulk of Protestant Christianity into the encounter of world religions will depend on how acceptable his Christology is to other theologians as well as to lay Christians. As we have pointed out, his Christology is the basis of his concept of final revelation and also of his prime polar tension between that which is concrete and that which is universal. However, his view of Jesus as the Christ, while in the train of the logos theology of the early church, seems much too vague to allow the historical Jesus Christ to be as significant as he is for most Christians. Particularly in his last years, Tillich seemed to transform a flesh-and-blood God-man into a principle of negation of the concrete. This charge, however, must be substantiated.

The problem does not involve Tillich's term for Jesus as the "New Being." To use the term "being" of God and of Jesus Christ has some decided advantages in relating to mystics of all religions or to Hinduism, Buddhism, Taoism, and other religions that may use a similar ontology. Nor is the problem the fact that the logos points to a revelatory reality rather than to revelatory words. Jesus Christ *was* "transparent to the divine mystery," to use Tillich's phrase. Furthermore, some difficulties might also be minimized. For instance, while Tillich's identifying salvation and revelation with each other might not do justice to the many forensic and sacrificial passages of the Scriptures, there are many passages that tie salvation to a man's being "in Christ." And, there were many who "saw" who Jesus was, such as Peter and Paul, who immediately experienced the change of life and the wholeness that salvation implies. Therefore, it makes some good sense to say that the history of revelation and the history of salvation are the same history. However, the criticism of Tillich's Christology rests upon the way Jesus as the Christ negates all that is concrete in him.

Three significant passages from Tillich's writings will demonstrate what we feel is lacking in his Christology. First, in his *Systematic Theology*, there are several sections that show the impossibility of making anything definite out of the life of Jesus. As a sample, this will suffice:

The words of Jesus and the apostles point to this New Being; they make it visible through stories, legends, symbols, paradoxical descriptions, and theological interpretations. But none of these expressions of the experience of the final revelation is final and absolute in itself. They are all conditioned, relative, open to change and additions.[25]

This seems to be a very dubious way of taking the piece of history that involved the life of Christ, using it to experience the New Being, and then negating it as if it did not matter.

Perhaps the difficulty is that we need a language that can indicate "absolute events" without turning these into a form of idolatry. Not having such a language, however, we are left with the unhappy alternative of using terms like "sacred history," where "sacred" undermines the reality of "history."

A second quotation is in *Christianity and the Encounter of the World Religions*. The context is Tillich's attempt to show how universal the Christian faith has been in most periods of its history, affirming revelatory experiences in non-Christian religions while denying its own particularity. He writes:

Although the Fourth Gospel speaks more clearly than the others of the uniqueness of the Christ, it interprets him at the same time in the light of the most universal of all concepts used in this period, the concept of the Logos, the *universal principle* of the divine self-manifestation, thus freeing the interpretation of Jesus from a particularism through which he would become the property of a particular religious group.[26]

In line with this statement, Tillich interprets Jesus' famous words "You, therefore, must be perfect, as your heavenly Father is perfect" to read "You must be all-inclusive as your heavenly Father is all-inclusive." This too seems to distort the meaning of Jesus Christ. It makes a difference how you say that the interpretation of Jesus should be free from particularism. If you mean free from a narrow denominational interpretation, that is one thing. If you mean freedom from any historical anchor point, that is another. In the latter case, the concrete happening of the Christ event is gone. Tillich is too close to the latter use of freedom and therefore is far from the typical Christology of the Christian church.

One final quotation must suffice. In his article in *The Christian Century* entitled "How My Mind Has Changed," he says that his observations of Zen strengthened his theological conviction that the concept of religion in its larger sense "transcends the concrete existence of any religion, as God transcends each of his manifestations." [27] He feels that many educated people prefer Zen because of their aversion to objectified and literally interpreted Christian symbols. Therefore, Christianity must rid itself of all elements of a Jesulogical faith in favor of Christological faith, and then the East might be more receptive to it. If Christianity critically applies the criterion of "a faith which transcends every finite symbol of faith," it will enter into fruitful conversation with the East. These three quotations, which could be multiplied at length, sound as if Tillich has finally freed Christianity from its obsession with history. The *skandalon* has apparently been removed. And yet, is it ever a proper interpretation of the life and death of Jesus Christ to say that this concrete existence was being negated so that the followers of Christ might be better equipped for interfaith dialogue? We think not. There is a docetic or adoptionist strain in Tillich whereby he makes the absolute (or the ontological principle) far more important than Jesus' concrete existence. Tillich, of course, confesses his skepticism of historical knowledge, and constantly uses the term "picture" or "image" when referring to Christ, just as Hermann before him. But, picture of what? And is it the picture or the concrete historical reality behind the picture that is important?

It is interesting that Bonhoeffer, who is more often mistakenly thought of as an iconoclast than as a constructive theologian, has some acute observations to make concerning the historical Christ.[28] He maintains that dogmatics needs to be certain of the historicity of Jesus Christ, else the church is doomed. However, for Bonhoeffer, such certainty does not arise from history itself, since history does not give birth to absolutes. Rather, the certainty of Jesus' historicity is given by the miracle of his presence, the Risen One, which leads the church to confess him as the Historical One. Thus, the historicity of Jesus Christ requires the twofold aspect of history and faith, but from this confessional point of view the historic Christ remains permanent, not to be transcended in favor of a higher principle.

Where, then, shall we leave Tillich if we reject the final statement of his Christology? Unfortunately, no clear answer can be given from a systematic point of view except to deny the possibility of a closed system. This is not the day when either philosophy or theology can give to everything a consistent all-embracing explanation. Just as Kierkegaard rebelled against the system of Hegel, so all the disciplines that are caught up in Tillich's comprehensive system will rise up and protest that their academic subject has been put in too small a container. Yet just because a system is rejected qua system does not mean we must reject the valuable insights that the system tries to hold together. Nor is it necessary to reject the efforts toward a system. So much of modern theology is a piecemeal enterprise these days, related neither to the full spectrum of theological concerns nor to world religion, that it is refreshing to have a man like Tillich make the attempt to create a coherent system. It is a major task of the future to be taken up by encyclopedic minds, to try to see life and see it whole. But meanwhile the problem remains of assimilating the vast material pouring in from all the world religions and from our own secular culture, and of *beginning* the systematic program by witnessing to the centrality of Jesus Christ. It may be, as we believe, that such a beginning will always foreshadow the breakdown of a complete, intellectually respectable system. However, the alternative is to forget the *skandalon* of the incarnation, in which case there would be a far more disastrous breakdown of the tension between intelligibility and soteriology.

Tillich has borne good witness to the centrality of Jesus Christ for the Christian community. A casual reading of his answers to the student questions at Stanford University would reveal this.[29] He has been the constant critic of various forms of idolatry whereby we have worshiped the creed or Scripture more than the God behind them. He has also given a way of revitalizing the logos theme so that all the Biblical supports of exclusivism are given a mysterious depth. He has shown a way to conditional exclusivism, whereby we can affirm faith in Jesus Christ while being open to the latent Christ beyond Western Christianity. However, there is a dangerous Scylla and Charybdis in using the logos theme that neither Tillich nor Kraemer quite negotiates. On the one hand it is possible for Christology to be reduced to a brief segment of world history—the logos *en sarx* which then sits in final judgment on all other history. Such reduction is the fault of Barthian-type theologians. Or, it is possible for history to be reduced to a beatific vision, which has no more support than the smile of the Cheshire cat. This reduction is the fault of theologians like Tillich. Somewhere in between is more acceptable ground, where the tension between the logos *en sarx* and the logos *en archē* will not be denied.

Part Two

PRACTICAL IMPLICATIONS

VI

Theological Openness and the Mission of the Church

While we have used Kraemer as a foil against which to present arguments for a more inclusive theology, the question comes as to what such a theology means for the mission of the church. This question seems to arise in a natural way, especially since Kraemer's first book was a preparation for the Tambaram World Missionary Conference of 1938. Then, too, it is on the mission field that the frontier between religions is most felt. This is changing, of course. With every decade there are more Asians living in the West, bringing their faith with them. There is also a growing missionary drive being carried out in Europe and the United States by non-Christian religions.[1] However, for the moment, the first line of the meeting is still the mission field. Therefore, it is important to ask what the missionary groups have been doing since Tambaram. Has there been a tightening of the defense of the Christian faith, through fear of losing ground? Or has the oneness of the world and the resurgence of world religions produced a rethinking of theology, so that ecumenical relationships can be formed with other religions?

It can be substantiated that so far as the Protestant missionary councils are concerned, the years following Tambaram and up to 1958 were not great ones for rethinking of the Christian faith in relation to other religions. The development of any theological base whereby to treat other religions with fairness was postponed in favor of what was called "immediate practicality." A proof of this affirmation can be found in the Bossey document of the World Council of Churches (1958).[2] In this important paper there is a twofold confession, both that Christian theology since 1938 had not been related to missionary questions and also that the world religions had not been studied as living faiths able to function in the complexities of the modern world. Kraemer is a notable exception to this judgment in that he had been grappling with theology and the Christian mission throughout those twenty years of intellectual sterility. He had also been the constant critic of mission boards that substitute zeal and goodwill for scholarly competence. Apart from Kraemer, it is only after 1958 that there has been a decided progress beyond Tambaram.

One element, however, in the period between 1938 and 1958 ought not to be underestimated in its effect upon the theological underpinning of the missionary enterprise. This is the ecumenical movement itself. The significance of this movement is obvious. First of all, it revealed the inadequacy of dividing the church's mission into "home" and "foreign." Both the International Missionary Council and the WCC united churches from around the world, the so-called "younger churches" and the old-line European churches. The full fruit of this merger is only partly in evidence. To date, as indicated above, few of our major theologians have related their work to the resurgent non-Christian religions. However, the day is not far away when such domestic theologies will be too provincial to endure. With the IMC now a part of the WCC and called the Commission on World Mission and Evangelism, such provincialism will be thrown continually under the demand for a wider perspective.

Then, too, the merging of the two streams of mission and ecumenical relations has put the missionary motive and goal within the thinking of all churches, even of the orthodox communions that have not traditionally been evangelical in approaching the world. This has not been an easy confluence. For one thing, mission theology itself has been very unsettled. At the Willingen Conference of the IMC in 1952, with the theme "The Missionary Obligation of the Church," there were so many diverse opinions that no united report was possible as to what that mission was! The Ghana Conference of 1958 reformulated the question, so that it read: What does it mean in theological terms and practice, in this ecumenical era, for the church to discharge its mission to the world? A decision was made to hold experimental group meetings in different parts of the world in which theologians and practical workers might interact. It was from this meeting also that two men were commissioned to write books that might clarify mission theology. The result was to be Johannes Blauw's *The Missionary Nature of the Church: A Survey of the Biblical Theology of Mission*,[3] and D. T. Niles's *Upon the Earth: The Mission of God and the Missionary Enterprise of the Churches*.[4] However, the point at issue was whether the unsettled state of mission theology would be submerged in the more cumbersome machinery and all-embracing theological interests of the WCC. There was a further problem. Missionary thinking since Tambaram (1938) had centered in the doctrine of the church, which emphasis was congenial to the less evangelical communions within the WCC. To some leading missionary statesmen this was beginning to seem inadequate, since questions were constantly being raised about God's action in the world outside the church. Would the merger of the IMC and WCC smother this continuing examination of the missionary enterprise as many, such as Stephen Neill and Lesslie Newbigen, feared? It is too early to make any predictions. However, the theme of the New Delhi meeting where the merger occurred, "Jesus Christ the Light of the World," gave indication that the "larger Christ" may play a more important part than ever before in the theology of the encounter between Christian faith and non-Christian faiths. It also indicated that no church in the WCC could avoid problems associated with missionary outreach.

Another aspect of the ecumenical movement is important. This is the growing uniformity of approach to Christian theology that has accompanied the coming together of the major Protestant denominations. In whatever dialogue issues between religions, it will be a help if there emerges—as there certainly seems to be emerging—a predominant theological approach to the mission of the church. Today, even where there are marked differences of opinion, these are set off by common study documents and discussions. For instance, the author sent a letter to the heads of mission boards of five leading denominations—Baptist, Episcopal, Methodist, Lutheran, and Presbyterian—asking for a brief bibliography of the books that were most influencing their denomination's mission policy. In each case the same books were recommended! This is all to the good in giving a basic uniformity around which the expected diversity can cluster.

One warning against oversimplification must be given, however. The WCC, even with the inclusion of the IMC, does not include the many independent churches. Gerald Anderson points out that these independent evangelicals have been a constant source of missionary effort in the twentieth century and that today approximately one third of the total Protestant missionary endeavor is administered by agencies rooted in this tradition, although those agencies do not cooperate with either the WCC or the IMC.[5] Such evangelicals have been the stronghold of the exclusivist position, usually without either the depth or the erudition of Kraemer. They usually argue for the plenary inspiration of the Scripture and, among other things, are apt to believe in a literal hell to which men without Christ, both those who have rejected him and those who have never heard of him, are doomed.[6] Because of this strong exclusivism in the church, an exclusivism that should be distinguished from that of Kraemer, it is impossible to say that the WCC speaks for all Protestant Christians.[7] However, in any discussion in this book as to how the church is reacting to other faiths, we are thinking more of churches cooperating with the WCC, admitting that this approach is partial at best.

How far the ecumenical movement will go remains to be seen. It is certainly producing greater solidarity among the main-line denominations. And it is bringing a healthful criticism to bear upon the sanctity of religious organization. By and large, Christian theologians agree that Christianity as a religious system is as fully under the judgment of God as other religious systems. This means that organizations and thought systems are not quite the stumbling blocks to interreligious discussions that they once were. Interestingly enough, both Tillich and Kraemer would agree on this point. However, the type of theological openness under discussion in this book does have some practical implications, which might be called "paths for the future." Three of these are selected: What does theological openness mean in relation to the way Christianity is structured? What is the meaning of the much-discussed term "dialogue"? and finally, Is the word "conversion" serviceable when the sharp line between Christian faith and non-Christian faith is removed?

1. A REEXAMINATION OF THE STRUCTURE OF WESTERN CHRISTIANITY

W. E. Hocking has observed a basic difference between Western Christianity and Asian religions. The former has a precise structure, with a definite organization, a definite mission policy, a definite set of doctrines, standard of membership, schedule of activities, and so forth. In the East, there is no precise structure, and belonging to a religious group does not have the same clear-cut significance. A good example of this is to be found in the religious census of any Asian country. For instance, if the population is 140 million, the numerical list showing the adherents to the various religions might total 250 million.[8] The reason for the discrepancy is that Asians can think of themselves as Confucians and Buddhists at the same time, whereas Westerners have a hard time getting beyond denominational labels to the bigger term "Christian." The very words "organization" and "constituency" have a Western flavor to them.

It is not by chance that preciseness in doctrine and preciseness in church structure go together. Exclusive theology simply carries this Western tendency to the limit and draws a clear-cut line between who is a Christian and who is not. If there should be a deepening of our understanding of the nature of Christ beyond all creedal formulations, one of the practical outcomes should be a blurring of the lines of distinction—not only between Baptist and Presbyterian but also between Christian and Buddhist, Christian and Hindu, and so forth. This is not to give up the Western organizational pattern, nor to give in to the relativism of Symmachus. Rather, it is the admission that many church lines are manmade and have been drawn as a result of definite historical situations rather than by divine fiat. It is also the realization that there may be many in the East and in the West who will sit down in the Kingdom before those who consciously speak the name of Jesus Christ with all the New Testament meaning given to that name. A. C. Bouquet, for instance, has reportedly asked whether there could not be Christian Buddhists and Christian Hindus in the same sense that there were Christian Platonists.[9] And Kaj Baago, the church historian at the United Theological College in Bangalore, gives modern examples such as Brahmabandhav Upadyay and Manilal Parekh, who call themselves Hindus even while being baptized Christians. They continue to accept Hindu culture and thinking insofar as it does not conflict with their commitment to Jesus Christ.[10] Another well-known example of the same temperament was Sadhu Sundar Singh.

To de-emphasize the importance of the institutional church would throw the church-centered missionary movement into a turmoil, and apart from necessary theological discussion, the de-emphasis would be reckless. Furthermore, despite the fact that Christianity's organizational pattern is a Western product and that its mission has seldom survived with a casual organization, there are also theological issues that must be discussed in much more detail than a logos approach includes. For instance, what is the appearance and structure of the called-out people of God? If kerygma is a call to decision, to what is the decision and for what purpose? And what of the Sacraments? There have been, and are, all varieties of interpretation of the Sacraments, and these interpretations have been conditioned by the culture of the day. But no Protestant theologian is willing to admit that they are simply a function of *Historie*. Rather, they are dominical, and yet related to the institutional church at the same time. Therefore it would be wrong to suggest that the way Christianity is organized and lined off by doctrines is of no use. However, granted all this, the necessity of structure and the theological basis of structure must not become a wall to prevent the free exchange between Christianity and world religions.

There are two books that from entirely different fields attack the ecclesiastical definiteness of the Christian church. One, in the field of theology, is J. C. Hoekendijk's *The Church Inside Out*;[11] the other is W. C. Smith's *The Meaning and End of Religion*,[12] which is written from the field of *Religionswissenschaft*. The title of Hoekendijk's book is itself a protest against church-oriented thinking. In a characteristic statement, he says:

Church-centric missionary thinking is bound to go astray, because it revolves around an illegitimate center. . . . The church-centrism, *which apparently is the only undisputed missiological dogma since Jerusalem in 1928*, has such a grasp on us that we don't even notice anymore how our thinking has become completely "ecclesiasticized." . . . Would it not be a good thing to start all over again and try to understand what it really means when we quote and requote our favorite missionary text, "The gospel of the Kingdom will be proclaimed throughout the oikoumene"—attempting to rethink our ecclesiology within this framework of Kingdom-gospel-apostolate-world? [13]

Hoekendijk rebukes the church for forgetting the "fourth man." [14] The "third man" is the product of classical and Christian civilization. He may be outside the church, but he is still associated with the Christian tradition and can be addressed by the usual Christian terms and organization. The significance of the new day is that this "third man" is less and less in evidence. In his place there is the "fourth man," who is in opposition and is "outside" both the church and the church-created ethos. This man is producing the "post-Christian," "post-ecclesiastical," "post-bourgeois" era. Hoekendijk draws two conclusions from this: first, that the professional churchman can in general no longer be the best-suited organ for the apostolate; second, that the organs of the apostolate will have to distanciate themselves as far as possible from everything that looks "church." Instead of a church-oriented mission, Hoekendijk advocates a freedom from all established patterns so that the layman (not the professional) can be scattered through his world as a Christian *presence*.

The ferment of this kind of thinking has been great in the Western world, as evidenced by the variety of new ministries in the past ten years, particularly in urban centers. Perhaps the structure of the entire parish system will have to be rethought in ways that are not explicitly recognized at the moment. This is what Hoekendijk implies, particularly when it is outreach that is being discussed. He writes:

It is generally recognized that the parish type of congregation may still have significance in our day for the "preserving" pastorate, but that, generally speaking, it is not well suited for the "outreach" and the apostolate. . . . A church that wants indeed to be pro-existent—to be there for the other—can therefore never be organized exclusively in local parishes.[15]

If this line of thought proves valuable for the Western world, in which the clear-cut lines between church and world are blurred for the sake of mission, it should also affect the entire frontier where Christian faith meets other faiths. For example, the *International Review of Missions* during the last two years has been carrying on a running debate over the importance of the institutional church—whether the order of movement should be "God-church-world," in which the organized church would mediate the grace of God to the world; or whether the order should be "God-world-church," in which Hoekendijk's thesis would be given universal validity.[16] However, even assuming that Hoekendijk represents the wave of the future, two warnings need to be spoken. One is that new patterns that break down compound walls and the definite lines between church and world are not known in advance, nor are they dreamed up in New York office buildings for the rest of the world. The Christians of Asia and Africa, who sense the infinite variety in Jesus Christ, must also lead the way in the "post-colonial" era of missions. The other warning is that the Christian *presence* in the world, which is encouraged by logos Christology, easily develops in a one-sided way unless it is balanced by an emphasis on redemption and vicarious suffering. Wilhelm Andersen, for instance, expressed gratitude that the World Missionary Conference at Willingen (1952) laid such stress on the crucified and risen Lord.[17] As he put it, a one-sided incarnational theology such as is prominent in Anglican circles (and in Hoekendijk) can conjure up great misunderstanding by suggesting that the sole task of the church is solidarity with the world and some form of social gospel. There is always, says Andersen, a tension between incarnation and redemption, between logos *en sarx,* and the logos, who—*en sarx*—"died for our sins according to the Scriptures." As long as the tension is maintained, then Hoekendijk's disparagement of the institutional church is more a point of emphasis than a complete denial of its worth. These two warnings, however, one against preplanning the structure of the dispersed people of God and the other against a rejection of the kerygma—should not dull the force of Hoekendijk or of the criticism that theological definiteness and ecclesiastical exclusiveness usually go together, to the detriment of the Christian faith.

The other book that points in the same direction, though from a completely different field of scholarship, is W. C. Smith's *The Meaning and End of Religion*. Smith, who has served as a missionary and now as one of our foremost scholars in *Religionswissenschaft,* is opposed to the way in which religions are set off from one another and conceptualized into theoretical entities, and then defended or attacked as if they were walled cities. He urges that we give up the quest for the essence of religion. In fact, he feels that the noun "religion," suggesting as it does a clearly defined unit, should be dropped completely in favor of two other terms: "cumulative tradition" and "faith." Cumulative tradition would be open to historical research and the comparative sciences. It is the area of comparative religion. What would be studied is no essence out of which spring a variety of imperfect historical forms. Rather, the study would be of the changing manifestations that can neither be marked off by the judgments of true or false nor be offered as descriptions of what it means to be a Christian (or a Muslim, or a Buddhist). Faith, on the other hand, is the existential relationship that a man may bear to God. When faith is present, then the many apologetic means for defending one religion against another are brought to an end. As Smith says:

The end of religion, in the classical sense of its purpose and goal, that to which it points and may lead, is God. Contrariwise, God is the end of religion also in the sense that once He appears vividly before us, in His depth and love and unrelenting truth, all else dissolves; or at least religious paraphernalia drop back into their due and mundane place, and the concept of "religion" is brought to an end.[18]

The defense that Smith makes of this thesis is a historical examination of the way the word "religion" has been used. His main conclusion is that its use as a noun, marking off one religion from another, was a very late development, centering chiefly in the Scholastic period following the Reformation. Before that time, there was fluidity in the use of the term, and more often words such as "faith," "piety," "reverence," "devotion," were used to characterize the Christian faith—words, incidentally, that have no plurals. Even Augustine's *De Vera Religione* is not what the title suggests, namely, a defense of Christianity as a specific religion against other world religions. The title should be translated *On Proper Piety* or *On True Religion* or *On Genuine Worship* and not *On the True Religion*. Religion, for Augustine, was no system of observances or beliefs, nor a historical tradition that was institutionalized and capable of outside observance. Rather, it was a vivid, personal confrontation with the splendor and love of God. There were, however, two developments that were to influence the exclusivism of later centuries. On the one hand, Augustine was giving words that could later be applied to the Christian institutionalized religion. On the other, since he was a Platonist, he was suggesting on a serious scale, and for the first time in Christian history, that there is an essence, or ideal, that transcends all particular apprehensions of religion, and that it was the historic Christ who made this ideal known. This seed thought did not bear fruit, according to Smith, until after the Reformation; and he summarizes by saying, "Throughout the whole Middle Ages, no one, so far as I have been able to ascertain, ever wrote a book specifically on religion." [19] In fact, the earliest that he found a religion named in the West other than Christianity was in the nineteenth century: "Boudhism" (1801), "Hindooism" (1829), "Taouism" (1839), "Zoroastrianism"

(1854), "Confucianism" (1862), and so forth.[20] The naming
of Christianity as a religion over against others did not pre-
cede the nineteenth century by much. Neither Zwingli nor
Calvin used the term "Christianity" at all, and Luther pre-
ferred the term "faith." Only with later men such as Hugo
Grotius and Lord Herbert of Cherbury, who tried to devise
a method for assessing whether a religion were true or false,
did the modern use of the word "religion" become established. The romantic movement of the nineteenth century
added the thought of religions' having a history and origin,
pushing into the background the predominant use of this
word in Christian centuries as relating to an existential encounter that was deeper and more significant than anything
that could be said about it.

The conclusion that Smith reaches is, as we have already
indicated, that the term "religion" should be dropped.[21] It
is inadequate for the man who believes and it is misleading
for one who does not. The Christian faith to the believer is
not one of the religions of the world. Neither is the faith of
any other believer to him. How little can a systematic approach, typical of books on world religions, really describe
vital faith? He states the matter forcefully in relation to
Islam.

Being a Muslim means living in a certain context, sociological,
historical, idealogical, and *transcendent*. . . . The concern of the
observer with something that he calls *Islam* shifts attention from
the heart of the matter, namely people's living within this context,
to the context itself; which disrupts the whole procedure still
farther by omitting from his purview the context's transcendence.
It does this not perversely but inherently; since the observer by
the very fact of being an outsider, a non-acceptor of the context,
has ruled out its transcendent quality in theory *a priori*. He has
conceptualized what for the man of faith does not exist; namely,
a context for his life shorn of its most significant dimension.[22]

Smith feels that where there is the division of religion into
cumulative tradition and personal faith, both the context

and the reality of each religion can be dealt with more adequately.

Here we will arrest the study of Smith's book. For several reasons, his thesis seems to touch our own. By his scholarly analysis of the use of the noun "religion," he has given historical support for saying that in most Christian centuries, theologians did not consider Christianity a reified entity, marked off by doctrines and organization from the "outside" world. This is an answer from history to theologians of exclusivism. At the same time, Smith has given a way of speaking about the historical movements we call world religions as well as the saving contact with the living God, which is the concern of exclusivism. By his term "faith," recognition is given to the vital heart of religion—to Barth's "Wholly Other," or Otto's *Das Heilige,* or Tillich's question of "ultimate concern," or Eliade's description of the "sacred." By his phrase "cumulative tradition," the possibility is given of studying the rich variety that all religions afford without stumbling over the truth claims of each of them. This is openness in the most liberal sense.

It is probably true that, as E. L. Allen observes, an individual is constantly moving back and forth between commitment to one religion and detachment from that commitment for the sake of scientific study. It is also no doubt true that in studying religions, by the exercise of imaginative sympathy disciplined by intellectual rigor, one can sense the faith element as well as the historical tradition in another's mind and heart. However, when that happens, the resultant dialogue involves the meeting of persons rather than of religious organizations. Organizations with bylaws and doctrines do not hold dialogue. People do that—"we" speaking to "you" about "us," to use Smith's expression. Such an emphasis brings Smith close to Hoekendijk. By the latter's questioning of the well-defined institutional church, and the former's questioning of the well-defined Christian religion, both seem to be breaking down some artificial, man-made barriers so that interfaith traffic can continue to flow. This is as it should be. It is not the rejection of structure that is our goal, since this is neither possible nor desirable. Rather, it is the rejection of the *emphasis* on structure that is desired. It is when structure is deified that Christian flexibility has been lost. Then interfaith encounter is paralyzed before it is begun.

2. A REEXAMINATION OF DIALOGUE

If the approach to revelation be such as was indicated throughout this thesis: i.e.,

if we only know the absolute relatively,

if there is an inherent weakness in propositional truth, so that much of the language used in religion is "hinting speech,"

if the goal of the devotee to a revelation is to know an ultimate reality who/which saves, rather than to accumulate systematic knowledge,

if the logos *en archē* deepens with mystery the presentation of the Logos *en sarx,*

then the theological method of dealing with other religions must always be that of dialogue. The attitude that has characterized exclusivism, in which a body of truth is fully known and able to be communicated so as to displace all previously held religious beliefs, is monologue. It is an anachronism, even where it still motivates missions. In its place there must be a constant and continuing dialogue with men of other faiths.

However, the word "dialogue" is a slippery term. The biennial council meeting of the Christian Institute for the Study of Religion and Society recently studied the nature and basis of dialogue and concluded that while nobody was against it, there were many contradictory notions held about it. For some, it was an end in itself—conversation for conversation's sake. For others, it was a quest for truth, divine truth, which may prompt the Christian to reconsider not only his communication of such truth but also his own grasp of it. For still others, it was merely an effective evangelistic tool.[23] Because of this ambiguity in the term, let us outline a few of the premises upon which legitimate dialogue must proceed:

a. *The ability to listen.*[24] In 1958, at the Ghana Assembly of the IMC, one of the outstanding addresses was by a Burmese Christian, U Kyaw Than, who complained that the Christian missionaries to his country, by and large, had failed to listen, particularly to the resurgent Buddhist religion.[25] He pointed out that in Burma, the missionaries attribute the renascence of Buddhism to a revived nationalism or a cultural renewal. But this quick judgment is made oftentimes by Christian workers who do not know a word of the classical Pali, and who could not understand a profound book in Burmese or the expositions of Buddhism that were then going on in the Buddhist Council Sessions at Rangoon. The renascence, said Than, is a theological one, and there must be what he called a "theological penetration" of the Buddhist system if we are to understand the present situation. A Buddhist theologian, he continued, is expected to know fifteen canonical books, plus eight standard reference books for each of the fifteen. These undergird Burmese culture and society. In 1819, Adoniram Judson, one of the first Western missionaries to Burma, was one of the few who realized that to converse with the Buddhist, it is necessary to know these works too. However, since then, the missionary has tended to write off Buddhism by calling it a cultural phenomenon, and then to make his concentration of effort in the relatively easy area of the hill tribes. Than concluded his criticism by saying that we need more of a mind-to-mind encounter, which involves listening to the theological core of Buddhism rather than continuing a one-way proclamation coupled with a *Diakonia* resembling a watered-down technical assistance program.[26]

There is a good example of listening in a recent visit of Winston King to Burma. During the twenty months he was there, he found himself confronted again and again with the fact that Theravada Buddhism flatly denies the existence of a Supreme Being in any form, and yet the adherents undeniably had "some sense of a luminous experience of the transcendent," just as he had. This led him to ask what it was that functioned as a substitute for God. He found his answer not in any one single Buddhist term, but in four: *dharma* (law, truth; intimating cosmic order), *karma* (the law of cause and effect; intimating moral order), *Nirvana* (the supreme goal; utterly transcendent, utterly real and utterly desirable), and *Buddha* (the Enlightened One, the Revelator and also the Example, fulfilling a role comparable to that of Jesus, the Christ). These four terms, King suggests, constitute "a four-fold reality complex" that fulfills a God function in Buddhism.[27] King gave his hypothesis a trial run in conversation with the Venerable U Thittila, a Buddhist scholar. They took the Christian hymn "Immortal, Invisible, God Only Wise," deleted the personal names and pronouns relating to God, and considered whether the hymn would make sense to Buddhists if the blanks were filled by Buddhist terms. With some hesitation, U Thittila agreed that the blanks could be filled, and moreover by one or other of the four terms constituting King's suggested reality complex.

There are a few considerations in the matter of listening, however. Who is to do the listening—and the consequent speaking? Many scholars who deal with this problem have an uncanny way of limiting the dialogue to scholars. It was W. E. Hocking who first called for what he termed "Watchtowers of Thought" where scholars of different religions might study together.[28] Kraemer agreed with this proposal and recommended that Western and Eastern leaders of the missionary enterprise place in the great non-Christian religio-cultural areas small bands of experts thoroughly trained in the respective religions and cultures of those areas. In the last decade, several such centers have arisen, of which the most productive to date has been the Christian Institute for the Study of Religion and Society in Bangalore, India, which began on October 17, 1957, under the able direction of the late Paul Devanandan.[29] One of the aims of this institute is to establish vital contact with non-Christian thought, to initiate conversation with those of other religions on living issues. However, as wise and as necessary as these "Watch-towers" are, the listening and response is probably as important and effective when done by the whole gamut of humanity who live on the border where faith meets faith—travelers, business people abroad, students in foreign universities, government employees, service personnel, plus the percentage of national Christians who live in close and continual encounter with non-Christians. Stephen Neill reminds us that 80 percent of Christians in younger churches are village dwellers. This indicates that the listening is not only an exercise among scholars, but also a contact across class and economic levels, and between those whose knowledge is mixed with a great amount of ignorance.

This proposition of Kraemer's and Hocking's which involves the importance of experts is open to one other reminder. An expert who has the tools to study other religions *and enter into their spirit* while committed to his own position is one thing. A dogmatic expert who is so sure of his own position that he knows the boundary line where his religion ends and someone else's begins is another. Kraemer's expert is of the latter sort. He is one who has a clear view of the creative center of his own and other religions (what the Germans call *Lebensmitte*), and he possesses this knowledge in such a clear and concise way that it is defended by apologetic rather than reworked by a plastic encounter.[30] However, if there is a depth to any theological statement, particularly statements like "God was in Christ," then the line of boundary might well be too indefinite to draw with scholarly precision. The use of the term "expert" or "scholar" often implies knowledge intact and complete, when actually, in the religious field, knowledge does not have this exactness at all. From scholar down to village peasant, knowledge and ignorance are blended. And along the same scale, the knowledge is not just that of factual completeness, but includes the element of saintliness. As D. T. Niles observed in an apothegm, "Religious truths do not meet in the library." Expertness includes the openness of the saint as well as the openness of the academician. It is our incompleteness, the "not as if I had already arrived or were already perfect" element, and the mystery of that with which we deal that makes listening an imperative.

One final consideration should be remembered. The purpose of the listening is not merely to learn about someone else's faith. It is this in part. But in part it is learning about ourselves too. This statement is made on the premise that there is no truth for the Christian, whether it be found in his own scheme of things or elsewhere, that is outside his commitment to Jesus Christ—who is the Way, the Truth and the Life.[31] It is not as though the Christian has a well-determined yardstick that can measure what fits the Christian scheme and what does not. It is rather that the Truth shades off into the mystery where men can say, "I know," yet without producing convincing proof. It is a case of "the deep responding to the deep." The Christian, in listening, attributes what he hears to the fullness of Christ. He knows with Paul that "all things are ours." Just as space science adds insights to the doctrine of creation, the knowledge of other religions adds insights to the doctrine of the logos. In the words of Kenneth Cragg:

It goes with the universality of the Gospel that every faith by which men have worn their humanity has a positive relation, however wistful, with the fullness of Christ.[32]

The listening, then, is not to some alien voice, nor to competing bodies of truth. The listening is to a voice that has a familiar accent—that can enrich our own understanding and then prompt the sharing of a fuller Christ.

b. *A conviction about the prevenience of Christ.* Underlying what has just been said is a conviction about the prevenience of Christ—that it is a reality and that it conditions every interfaith dialogue so far as the Christian participant is concerned. This conviction was most clearly expressed at the Third Assembly of the World Council of Churches at New Delhi (1961),[33] particularly in the section on witness. We will quote a few of the relevant paragraphs of this report, where the doctrine of the universal Christ was stated with the most clarity. We will use the same paragraph numbers as in the report itself.

Introduction

(1) Christ loves the world which he died to save. His is already the light of the world, of which He is the Lord, and His light has preceded the bearers of the good news into the darkest places. . . . *He is the universal Christ whom men dimly and uncomprehendingly discern amidst their gropings for the truth and righteousness.*[34]

(2) [Christians should] go forth into the 20th century world with joyful confidence knowing that the Holy Spirit will lead them to where Christ already is.

A. Jesus Christ: The Savior of the World

(13) Because God in Christ has reconciled the world to himself, we may no longer judge our brother man by ordinarily accepted standards. God has not condemned us: we may not condemn any man. . . . Joyfully we affirm our solidarity with all men.

(17) . . . The church is sent, knowing that God has not left himself without witness even among men who do not yet know Christ, and knowing also that the reconciliation wrought through Christ embraces all creation and the whole of mankind. . . . In the churches we have but little understanding of the wisdom, love and power God has given to men of other faiths and of no faith, or of the changes wrought in other faiths by their long encounter

with Christianity. We must take up the conversation about Christ with them, knowing that Christ addresses them through us, and us through them.[35]

These paragraphs, which were guided through committee by Indian theologians—notably P. Devanandan and M. M. Thomas—say a great deal, while leaving many questions unanswered. For instance, in what sense can it be said that "Christ has already sought" the non-Christian? or that "Christ comes toward the non-Christian person before the preacher"? It would be on safer and more traditional ground to say that the universal approach of Christ is only appreciated to the full by Christian and non-Christian in connection with the preaching of the gospel and the presence of the church.[36] There is also the unanswered question of the ultimate destiny of mankind, particularly those who are consciously outside of any commitment to Jesus Christ. This question might be phrased, What is the relation between the atonement and "the light that enlightens every man"? However, all of these questions are farther along the road of interfaith dialogue. The main point that is being made here is that the basis of interfaith dialogue is the activity of Christ "in with and under" the total humanity that God has created. We listen and converse, not simply because of a common humanity—an *ewig Menschlichkeit*—but because of the operation of a common Lord in his creation.

c. *An adjustment to the word "syncretism."* Several of the leading Indian theologians, notably D. T. Niles and Kaj Baago, have felt that the aversion of mission leaders to the ideas surrounding syncretism has reinforced a ghetto attitude in the Indian church. If that is so, then it is this ghetto attitude that must be challenged if dialogue is to be free and open. Yet it is understandable why theologians of the past few decades have looked askance at syncretism and refused to endorse any meaning of the term. For one thing, it seemed to mix so much base alloy in the Christian message that the door would open for all kinds of perversions of the Christian message, and the foundation of the mission enterprise would be weakened. Syncretism as a missionary problem began to be discussed in earnest at the Jerusalem Missionary Conference of 1928. At this conference, there was a call for indigenous Christianity, and the need to emphasize the spiritual heritage of the great Eastern cultures, particularly in the rising tide of nationalism. There were pleas from missionaries, especially Anglo-Saxon missionaries, to adopt a less dogmatic attitude toward non-Christian religions. To many others, however, this was a threat to Christianity's uniqueness and there was a consequent reaction from Western theologians who were fresh from the influence of Karl Barth. H. W. Schomerus, who occupied Warneck's chair of the Science of Missions at Halle, wrote a long contribution entitled "Der Syncretismus als Missionsproblem unter besonderer Berücksichtigung Indiens" in the second volume of his book *Indien und das Christentum*. The happenings in Nazi Germany, where so many Christians capitulated to the desires of the state, added additional odium to the word "syncretism." So did the reaction to one of the early conclusions of comparative religion, that Christianity was a syncretistic religion.[37] This reaction continues to be felt in men like Lesslie Newbigen, Visser 't Hooft, and particularly Kraemer. No other modern author has spent more time warning against the danger of syncretism than Kraemer.[38]

The issue as to whether one is for or against syncretism is primarily in the way it is defined. If it is defined as the conscious attempt to put together alien elements so as to have one religion, for whatever utilitarian motive—then, of course, it is an evil. If it is defined as putting faith in modern and relevant terms, then there is hardly an issue worth debating. However, if it means the reshaping and restating of Christian doctrine and practice in the light of new cultural settings and a continuing interfaith dialogue, then syn-

cretism, as so defined, must be accepted if there is to be freedom in the dialogue between Christian faith and other
faiths.

Kaj Baago makes a vigorous defense of syncretism in this
third sense.[39] The early church, he maintains, adopted and
absorbed elements from surrounding religions, "creating the
gigantic and wonderful syncretistic religion which came to
be called Christianity." [40] This primitive church described
Jesus in terms from philosophy and mystery religions.
Clement could quote from Plato and Aristotle. In worship
the church copied the initiation rites of Isis religion and
formulated a great many theological statements concerning
the Sacraments from concepts of the Mithras cult. This same
church depicted Christ in the form of pagan gods—as God's
zither player (Orpheus), as the true Apollo, or as Mithras
riding gloriously in his four-in-hand vehicle. The early
church took over pagan festivals, particularly the great sun
festival of December 25. In short, the Christian faith became indigenous. Yet, it did not deny the uniqueness of
revelation in history or say that the God who spoke in a
variety of ways could not speak decisively in one way. The
fear that Christianity's uniqueness will be imperiled is great
among those who write against syncretism. Baago tries to
show, with some success, that this fear is unfounded. His
conclusion is that the Greek-Christian syncretistic era has
given the modern church a much-needed example. "As the
first missionaries crossed Palestine's borders so we are today
to cross borders to other cultures and religions. In India, this
will mean a Hindu-Christian syncretism, with all its prospects and all its dangers." [41]

In some ways, Kraemer is not too far from this position,
even though he would prefer the more traditional mission
terms of "accommodation," "assimilation," or "adaptation"
to that of "syncretism." However, there is a basic error in
Kraemer, to which we pointed in Chapter III, which prevents the freedom that is necessary for dialogue. Let us

follow his argument. He says that in the encounter of religions, there must be a "penetrating insight into the creative center (*Lebensmitte*) of foreign religions and cultures,"
and a "realistic and adequate appreciation of how these foreign cultures and religions have coalesced with the heart,
mind and spontaneous attitude toward the life and the world
of the people that have been moulded by them." [42] Apparently, what Kraemer means is that however non-Christian
religions change in the modern period, the change is the
outgrowth of their "creative center." When they are planted
in other cultures, it is impossible that they avoid adaption
and change to fit the new environment, but the creative center is not altered.[43] However, apart from the fact that this
implies an essence in an outdated Platonic sense, the crux
of the issue is the way Kraemer defines the creative center
of Christianity. For non-Christian religions (which he calls
"foreign") the center was said to be indissolubly connected
with the cultural environment. This is why he often terms
these religions "humanistic." The center of the Christian
faith, on the other hand, is the "Biblical revelation," as if
this revelation could be described apart from the cultural
environment in which it existed and through which it has for
centuries been transmitted. The position of this thesis is that
there is no pure Biblical revelation that can be set off from
this historical situation. Therefore, there should be neither
fear of the word "syncretism" nor the delusion that doctrines
—even doctrines at "creative center"—will become altered
through dialogue and cross-cultural movement.[44]

d. *A stress on the personal element.* Whether or not the
participants in interfaith dialogue have a theology close to
Kraemer or to Tillich, it should be axiomatic that the essence
of dialogue involves people rather than religious systems.
People are always more than systems, just as God is always
more than any expression about God. Therefore, in the encounter of Christianity and Buddhism, for example, it would
be more proper to speak of the encounter of Christians and

Buddhists. "Systems of belief provide subject matter for discussion, but it is living faith that makes an encounter." [45] There are many signs that this important axiom is being taken more seriously. For instance, there are many books on world religions written in the last decade or so that are not so much collections of facts as attempts to empathize and to get inside another religion. Examples of this type might be Archer's *Faiths Men Live By,* or Huston Smith's *The Religions of Man,* or W. C. Smith's *The Faith of Other Men.* These are books in which the human element predominates over the statistical or informational.[46] In addition, there are many testimonies to a transformation of outlook through face-to-face encounters. For instance, Canon Howard Johnson wrote that after his recent travels, Buddhists, Muslims, and Hindus had become "people with piety and pain in their faces," something very different from what he had conceived in his earlier academic studies.[47] Underlying all the stress on the personal element in dialogue is the realization of the activity of God in Christ, whose love and atonement are not just preserved in the traditions of the Christian church but spill over the man-made boundaries between religions and "enlighten" every man.

There is a book that does not mention world religions at all and yet sets forth some elemental facts about dialogue. This book is Reuel Howe's *The Miracle of Dialogue,*[48] in which the author analyzes the dynamics of interpersonal and intergroup action and points out the barriers and the transformations that occur in dialogue. The author defines dialogue as "that address and response between persons in which there is a flow of meaning between them in spite of all the obstacles that normally would block the relationship." [49] In such a relationship, the participants "experience the other side," to use Buber's phrase, and each participant both informs and learns. For such dialogue to occur, it is not necessary for convictions to be watered down or laid aside. "The dialogic thinker . . . is willing to speak out of

his convictions to the holder of other convictions with genuine interest in them and with a sense of the possibilities
between them." [50]

So important is dialogue that Howe can state bluntly,
"Communicate or perish." Not only are information and
meaning conveyed, and not only is the basis given for people
to make responsible decisions (even where the decision is a
"no" to the communicator), but dialogue allows persons "to
be." [51]

Man becomes man in personal encounter, but personal encounter
requires address and response between person and person. Man
has dominion over the created world, and there is no limit there
that can bind him. But he cannot have dominion in the world of
the personal. . . . The person who stands over against him limits
him, and the other person cannot be removed, fathomed or ex-
ploited. . . . The person of the other demands, by his very existence, that he be acknowledged as a *thou* in his own right, as a
thou to my *I,* and as an *I* to himself. . . . I can only speak to
him and leave him free to respond, and out of that exchange we
may both be called forth as persons in a relationship of mutual
truth.[52]

Howe feels that this authentic and open meeting between
man and man cannot occur without an implicit meeting between man and God. "To really see another is to see the
Other, and to really love another is to love the Other." [53]

It is some such analysis as Howe's that owes much to
Buber's I-Thou as well as to Tillich's theology of ultimate
concern, which must be kept in mind in the continuing dialogue between the religions. There are two further insights,
however, in Howe's treatment that are very suggestive. One
is his distinction between dialogic method and dialogic principle.[54] The *principle* of dialogue is what has been discussed
—an openness to the other side, with a willingness not only
to speak but to be changed by what we hear. The *method*
is the servant of the principle. It may be a round-table discussion in a study center, but it can also be a lecture—or

even a sermon! The key is whether the lecturer is alert to and activates the meanings of his hearer in relation to what he is saying. The importance of making this distinction between method and principle is that sometimes the group process can be used as a clever way of manipulating people into a predetermined point of view. The outcome may look like an example of dialogue, when actually it is an example of brainwashing.

The second insight of Howe that bears on our thesis is the close connection he makes between theological exclusiveness and monologue. A statement in Howe's own words will suffice:

Unfortunately, many people hold and proclaim what they believe to be true in either an opinionated or defensive way. Religious people, for example, sometimes speak the truth they profess monologically, that is they hold it exclusively and inwardly as if there was no possible relation between what they believe and what others believe, in spite of every indication that separately held truths are often complementary.[55] The monological thinker runs the danger of being prejudiced, intolerant, bigoted and a persecutor of those who differ with him.[56]

There is really, then, no sensible option between monologue and dialogue—between radical displacement and theological openness. Communication alone is the way of life. "The most important thing about this dialogue between the church and the world (and therefore, between Christian and Buddhist, for example) is that God acts in and through it to influence both the church and the world and to judge, purify and transform both." [57]

e. *A commitment to "boundless communication."* This term "boundless communication" was put forth by Karl Jaspers, and is the counsel arrived at by E. L. Allen in his book, *Christianity Among the Religions.* Before dealing with Allen's meaning of this term, we should note the method he pursues. His standpoint is not that of a theologian but of a philosopher of religion. That is, his purpose is not to be apologetic or missionary, nor will he begin with the axiom that Christianity is final. Yet, and somewhat paradoxically, Allen wants to be a committed Christian who in his personal experience has sensed that Jesus Christ (not Christianity) is final. Allen is not content with the typical feeling of objectivity conveyed by so many philosophers and historians of religion—which feeling, incidentally, makes possible the historical relativism of Troeltsch and others. This raises the problem, however, as to how one can be at the same time a philosopher in search of truth from whatever source and a Christian committed to ultimate truth from one source.

He answers this problem of method by referring to experience. It is a matter of experience that we can alternate between commitment and detachment. Under the latter, we detach ourselves emotionally from the object of study, much as the phenomenological school tries to do. Personal knowledge is then transferred to concepts, which are put over against the concepts of other religions. Here the Buddhist, who also has detached himself from his faith for purposes of rational discussion, will state his objections to a personal God, and the Christian in turn will give his reasons for one —both arguing in love and with a passion for the truth. Unless the standpoint of observer can be held, there can be no rational discourse or comparison of religions at all. Yet this standpoint is not enough, else the only answer to the relation between religions is some form of relativism.

Side by side with the detached observer position can be a commitment to the absolute which is "truth for me" or "for us." Here Allen follows Karl Jaspers' *Vernunft und Existenz*, which develops the position that to recognize truth in other religions does not necessarily diminish the devotion to one's own truth. This is obviously an existential solution. When I face my neighbor's truth, I may wish to discourse rationally. But, in the face-to-face encounter, "boundless communication," I am changed too. I may (1) hold by truth more firmly, (2) abandon it because I have seen it is not true, or (3) recast it in the form of fuller and richer truth. On the plane of observer, I never reach *the* truth, but only observe conflicting claims to it. On the plane of participant, there is no truth save that to which I come, under the guidance of God and in relation of love to my fellows.

This double standpoint, which seems true to life and also to the claims of the various religions, is a most appealing one. It allows for the openness of the historian and the firmness of the dogmatist. It admits of conflict between religions, which conflict Allen does not minimize or gloss over. Yet it provides for communication. It even allows for a fair treatment of those truths of other religions which are based upon different presuppositions than Christianity. Many times the Christian must say of another's faith: "I cannot say that is true, nor can I say it is not true. Here are depths in the wisdom of God that must be further explored."

In order for the Christian to maintain this double viewpoint, there must be a theological basis in his faith, which Allen finds in the doctrine of the incarnation. He feels there are two possible interpretations of this doctrine, both of which conserve its crucial significance in the Christian faith. On the one hand, the revelation of God can be confined to a single stream of history, which arose in Israel. Under this position, exclusivism is born as well as the imperialism of the typical missionary call. The other interpretation is that what is revealed in Israel and in Christ may not be restricted but is a dealing of God in mercy with all men at all times. Under this position, an inclusive view of world religions is possible. This second interpretation of the incarnation is the one Allen favors, ruling out the first entirely. The interpretation is about the same as that described by Sebastian Franck and Schelling when they talk about the latent and manifest Christ.

Allen feels that his term "boundless communication" is very close to Hocking's "reconception," but is more dynamic. Also, Allen avoids the optimism of predicting a world faith, as well as the offensiveness of beginning (or finding quickly) that Christianity is superior to all others. What will come out of communication, no one can foresee. He does not envisage any syncretism in the bad sense of that word, nor assimilation, nor a world faith, but something better than these—mutual understanding.

f. *The acceptance of risk.* To be addressed by those of other faiths means that Christian convictions are as much open to examination and criticism as are the convictions of those to whom we speak. Furthermore, the Christian must be willing to change his conceptions and theological statement if the process of dialogue should indicate it. Convictions that will not stand up through the light of dialogue are not really convictions at all.

One excellent statement of the risk involved in dialogue is Douglas Steere's article "Mutual Irradiation." [58] Steere at first entertains the possibility that dialogue is an evangelistic tool to subdue others to faith in Jesus Christ. This he quickly rules out. But then he asks a disturbing question.

How can we be sure that in the course of the irradiation and reconstitution, the polarizing powers of the other great religions may not triumph in the end? How can we be sure that Christ, unless he is more dogmatically defended, will not end up as one more avatar in the Hindu pantheon, as a Great Galilean Bodhissatva in the Mahayana Buddhist hierarchy; or as a forerunner, even if the leading forerunner, to the prophet Mohommed.[59]

Steere's answer to this probing question is that there is no way around this danger. "Only a vulnerable Christ is viable." In fact, it is the acceptance of risk that is an indication of the vitality of the Christian faith.

Just in passing, it should be noted that Christianity seems at the moment to be far more open to the risks of dialogue than most other of the world religions, with the possible exception of Zen Buddhism. The most notorious resistance to dialogue is among Muslims. They have not allowed modern science or literary scholarship to affect interpretations of the

Koran, nor have they ever taken seriously Christianity's interpretation of itself. No less an Islamic scholar than W. C. Smith reports that: "The present writer knows no book by a Muslim showing any 'feel' for the Christian position; nor indeed any clear endeavor to deal with, let alone understand, the central doctrines." [60] This is echoed by Charles Malik, one of the most distinguished scholars of the Arabic-speaking Orthodox churches: "There is not a single Muslim scholar in all history, so far as I know, who has written an authentic essay on Christianity." [61] One of the fairest articles by an Islam scholar is Muhammad Kamel Hussein's "City of Wrong." [62] But even in Hussein's discussion of Good Friday, he does not break with Muslim tradition and say that Jesus really died, nor is he willing to admit that Jesus' disciples were simple fishermen.

As to Hinduism, its intolerant tolerance is not nearly so open as might appear. Kraemer is right when he says in a footnote: "An intriguing point in relation to the offence of 'exclusiveness' is always that the Hindus especially, in the name of 'inclusiveness,' are thoroughly exclusivists in a concealed way. That is, by their claim in regard to 'inter-faith relations and conversations' that 'inter-faith relations' should mean that the 'Christian arrogance' of offering by the Gospel the normative concept of religion should be dropped at the outset, and the tenet of the one, universal religion, hidden in all religions, should be taken as the normative concept. They have, of course, a perfect right to maintain this latter position, but it is really strange that they do not see how such a demand at the outset that one of the partners in the *inter*-faith relation should surrender his true position is arbitrary dogmatism and a frustration of genuine *inter*-faith relation; a flight from the real issue. This phenomenon, however, seems to be inherent in the position of the 'inclusivists.' " [63]

Zen Buddhism is not quite so cloistered as Islam or Hinduism, but even here the element of risk is often lacking. Sometime ago it was the author's privilege to sit in a class under a Zen master. While there was much communication underneath the words, there was no desire on his part to relate his concepts to either Hinduism or other forms of Buddhism, all of which leads to the observation that the desire for dialogue with the acceptance of risk is at the moment predominantly a Western desire.

So much for the importance of dialogue in the West and the presuppositions on which it rests. What specifically are the results of dialogue? This can be answered only in a fragmentary way, though the question can be asked in either of two directions. It might be asked how the world religions have been changed through contact with Christianity. Or it might be asked how Christianity has been changed through its contact with world religions. We are going to take only the second part of this question, and attempt to give a few illustrations of possible changes within Christianity.

One type of change is the calling forth by other religions of latent teaching in the Christian faith. It is probably true of any religion that the full range of doctrine and insight is never alive in its fullness in any one generation. Different historical times bring up for discussion different aspects of the total truth. In recent decades, the church has been paying particular attention to parts of the Biblical revelation that indicate the oneness of the church, just as in other scholastic centuries, the differences were magnified. It stands to reason, therefore, that in an age of increasing contact between faiths, the non-Christian faiths will call forth aspects of the wide gamut of Christian belief that relate to Christianity's universalism. Huston Smith points to the type of thing we mean.[64] He refers to a Japanese professor, Dr. Kishimoto, who expressed the feeling that Protestantism has an excellent ethic but is not a religion in the full sense of the term since the mystical element is so often lacking. Smith suggests that it may well be that Protestantism has placed too much emphasis on God's will and obedience to that will, to the neglect of other faith components. Perhaps prophetic faith has worked the exclusion of ontological faith, the holiness of the "ought" overcoming the holiness of the "is." This is close to an observation of Hocking that Buddhism can teach Christianity much about the enjoyment of the impersonal element of ultimate truth. The impersonal element belongs to what Hocking terms "the vast inner spaces of God's being." This suggestion, which these men see as coming from Buddhism, is not completely alien to the Christian scheme. Much of Tillich's theology—e.g., dealing with the "God above God"—relates to this insight. Yet it is an underplayed chord in Christendom. It is not too much to expect of the hundreds of unplayed chords, through dialogue and the movement of God's Holy Spirit, that they may yet be heard.

A second type of change is more subtle. It relates to all the changes of meaning that occur in the use of language. Even within one language there is quite a difference in connotation and feeling tone when a word is replaced by a synonym. This difficulty is magnified when one religion is translated into the language of another culture, producing slight and inadvertent shifts of meaning. Let an illustration suffice. It concerns a sermon by Kenneth Cragg given in a mosque.[65] The text for his sermon was taken from the Koran.

It is He who fashioned you from the earth and gave you empire therein: So ask of Him forgiveness and turn to Him penitently Surely the Lord is nigh. (Surah 11:61.)

We are not interested in the content of the sermon, but rather in Cragg's treatment of the text. He entered into the thought of Salih's message, just as he would do with a Biblical text. Throughout the sermon, many of the interpretations were phrased so that they would produce agreement by both Christian and Muslim. He wrestled with the problem of man's creaturehood, his God-given task of subduing the earth, his need for forgiveness in pursuing his task, his need for worship, lest the conquest of the many destroy the unity of the One. Where Cragg's specific Christian faith came through was in dealing with the question of whether forgiveness is by divine fiat, "effortless," as it were; or whether there is a need for a cross so as to overcome evil and allow God to continue as a unity. Cragg, of course, opts for the latter. It is the method of Cragg, however, more than the specifics that concerns us. He entered into the vital heart of another faith, in this case the scriptures of Islam, and brought his Christian perception to bear in a way that must have been good for both listener and preacher. For both, there would be the slight shifts of meaning, the breaking up of stable connotations, and efforts toward mutual understanding. It is possible that Cragg's view of the atonement was enriched and that his listeners' understanding of theodicy broadened. In either case, the subtle changes would be produced through the flexible nature of religious language. These changes have happened, and will continue to happen in countless ways all along the frontier where Christians speak and listen to men of other faiths. Whether such changes of theological meaning will lead to greater interfaith understanding remains to be seen, although it would be a logical prediction on the basis of belief in logos *en arché*.

One final type of change is not so subtle as that produced by the connotations and emotive power of words. This is the conscious attempt at theological reconstruction. As was said earlier, Tillich was in the process of doing this when he died. What he might have accomplished in terms of a total system related to the world religions is not possible to say. There are a few others, however, who are taking up the challenge. Some interesting approaches are being made by Indian theologians Kaj Baago and Raymond Panikkar, particularly in regard to the nature of Christ. Baago's major work has not yet appeared.[66] Panikkar has expressed his approach in a doctoral thesis published under the title of *The Unknown*

Christ of Hinduism. Both agree, however, that there needs
to be a revised Christology using some form of the logos concept of the early fathers.

Panikkar's thesis is that Hinduism and Christianity are
related, not as falsehood and truth nor as natural and supernatural but as potency and act, seed and fruit, symbol and
reality, desire and thing-in-itself. Panikkar makes the bold
affirmation (though not unique among Catholic theologians):
"When a Hindu is saved . . . he is saved by the grace of
Christ, and is incorporated into the supernatural order and
yet he may know nothing about Christianity." [67] In order to
explain this thesis, the author begins by characterizing the
encounter between the two religions. If, says Panikkar, the
encounter centers in the doctrinal sphere, the only possibility
is for the religions to coexist or to try to subdue each other.
But religions do not meet in the doctrinal sphere so much
as at a deep existential level—what he terms the "ontic-
intentional" level. The ontic-intentional level is the same for
both the Hindu and the Christian; in fact, it is the ontological meeting point of all religious people. It might be described as either the goal of existence or as union with the
absolute. A yogi calls it "pure isolation"; Buddhists call it
Nirvana. Christians, on the other hand, say that we all do
meet in God and that there is only one mediator between
God and man wherever the meeting occurs—Christ. "Christ
is already there in Hinduism in so far as it is a true religion." [68]

From one point of view, Panikkar's logos Christology is
not particularly novel. Thus, when he says that the Christian
attitude toward Hinduism is not one "of bringing Christ *in,*
but of bringing him *forth,*" many modern theologians could
be speaking, particularly those of the Anglican or Roman
Catholic point of view. The same could be said about Panikkar's dogmatic challenge to Christians "to reformulate what
God has done in Christ in other lands." Cuttat, or Bouquet,
for instance, whom we have already mentioned, would join

Panikkar in such an outlook. However, in at least two re-
spects, Panikkar seems to go beyond others. On the one
hand, he would like to say something positive about Hinduism in its own right while maintaining that the logos is at
work in it. The problem for Panikkar is how to define the
dictum "Outside the church there is no salvation," while allowing for such broad and indistinct activity of the logos.
It will be remembered that Cuttat ended by saying that all
who had been affected by the logos in other religions at the
"ontic-intentional" level had to confess in a conscious way
their allegiance to the historic Christ before they could be
saved. Panikkar rejects this solution. For him, "the church"
must not be identified with outer appearance, nor "the sacraments" identified with Baptism and the Lord's Supper. The
sacraments may be ordinary means by which God leads the
people of earth to himself. But there is a broader vision to
be maintained. Christ is not only the historical redeemer,
but the third Person of the Trinity—the only one, ontological, temporal, and eternal link between God and the world.
If Baptism and the Lord's Supper have the support of the
historical Christ, and are thus connected with the will of
God, could it be that there are other sacraments that are
supported by the eternal Christ and the triune God? Panikkar poses the question and answers it affirmatively. In his
words, "The good bonafide Hindu is saved by Christ, not
by Hinduism—but it is through the sacraments of Hinduism." [69]

Such a theology gives some meaning to the possibility of
there being Christian Hindus even though the basis for
making human judgments as to who these are has been
removed. There is no way of counting on organizing these
or of calling them forth. In this regard, Panikkar seems more
daring than many other logos theologians. However, the
second way Panikkar attempts to advance is by showing
that his thesis is really implied in the Brahma Sutra I, 1, 2,
in the Hindu description of how God is related to the world.

We shall not follow his intricate analysis, but indicate two of his conclusions. One is that in the relation between Brahma and God, the one being impersonal and the other personal, the mind must include both in describing the ultimate. When we search for the *ground* of things, we take up the anthropological thirst for unity. When we search for the *end* of things, we take up the search for the transcendence of the Father. Both ideas—one specifically Hindu and the other specifically Christian—point to the same reality. "The personal God without the corrective of Brahma may well become an anthropocentric idol." [70]

The second conclusion of Panikkar from his study of the Brahma Sutra is that Hinduism, in order to relate God and the world, requires Ishvara, who is a mediator not to be divorced from Brahma, and yet not identified with it. Ishvara performs in Hinduism the same function as the second Person of the Trinity in Christianity. Panikkar says:

The dogma of the Trinity would appear as the unsought for—and often indeed inopportune answer to the inevitable question of an ontic mediator between the one and the manifold. This, in my opinion, is not just a Vedantic problem; it is the *amr* of the Koran, the logos of Plotinus and the Tathagate of Buddhism. In Hinduism it is Ishvara. [71]

Panikkar notes the evolution of Ishvara from the position of a lesser deity who is seldom mentioned, to the prominence given him in the Bhakti schools, where he receives a Godlike devotion. Conversely, when the personal dimension of Ishvara grows in importance, Brahma seems to be mentioned much less. Obviously, in all this analysis, the author wants to equate the Ishvara of the Brahma Sutra with Christ, since there needs to be a link between God and the world, both as an explanation of unity and as the point at which salvation occurs. The author of the Brahma Sutra did not think of Christ explicitly; but again, as Panikkar so often insists, the dialogue with Hindus does not begin with the historicity of Jesus but with the nonhistoric logos.

This presentation of Panikkar is not intended to show his worked-out system. Nor does it even sketch the relation of the "unknown Christ" to the other doctrines of the Christian church. Further, it is not enough to say, as he does, that the eternal logos is to be stressed when speaking with Hindus more than the historic Christ. More needs to be written about the relation of the logos *en archē* to the logos *en sarx*. However, we present this much of his thought as an example of a conscious attempt in recent years to rewrite sections of Christian theology in the awareness that it has to speak directly to the conviction and theologies of other great religions.

3. CONVERSION: YES OR NO?

The last question relates to conversion. This subject has received attention recently from study groups of the WCC in which an in-depth Biblical and theological analysis has been undertaken.[72] Our concern is much more limited since it relates only to the following question: Given an open theology—one that makes room for the activity of God in Christ in every religion and in every person—is the Christian mission under obligation to convert individuals to a belief in Jesus Christ? Very close to this, but not the same, is the question of whether the Christian mission is under obligation to convert individuals to the *church* of Jesus Christ.[73] Both of these questions, particularly the latter, have provoked much criticism from both inside and outside the church.

Those who say no to the Christian obligation to preach for conversion can point to many circumstantial reasons for their answer; for instance, the militant attitude of Christianity, its unconscious ties with colonialism and with Western business expansion, its airs of superiority, and so forth. All these negative elements may be more of a caricature than a characterization of the expansion of the Christian faith. Nevertheless, they are often in the minds of missionaries and theologians when the word "evangelism" is mentioned, and they certainly loom large in the thinking of non-Christians. Who today would not feel a little embarrassed for Christianity at this remark of the Anglican Metropolitan in India, made at the turn of the century:

We are sapping the old civilization in India. We are killing the ancient religions of India. I do not say that the work of killing them will be soon accomplished, but it is inevitable and because it is inevitable it is the duty as it is the privilege of this country [Great Britain] to give India her own religion.[74]

And even as late as 1960, an American missionary in India announced publicly: "We are militant evangelists out to capture the villages for Christ. Our goal is 600,000 villages in ten years." [75] Such militant statements seem uncharitable, if not obsolete. Nowhere does the influx into the Christian church warrant such optimism. Canon Warren has spoken much more realistically when he commented, "We have marched around the walls of other religions the requisite number of times, but they refuse to come down." This fact, of the decreasing success of evangelism, only reinforces the "no" that many would like to say to it, and makes some theologians seek some less imperialistic meanings to the word evangelism. Even Hans Küng, the well-known Roman Catholic ecumenical theologian, reacts negatively to the need for conversion in the following peroration:

Outside the church no salvation: Can you keep on saying this when you look with honesty at the present time, and consider that of 2,500 million inhabitants of earth, only 847 million are Christians? . . . What have you to say about the salvation of these millions who live at the *present time* outside the Catholic church and altogether outside Christianity?

Outside the church no salvation: Can you keep on saying this when you look without prejudice at the past and consider that the years of humanity's existence before Christ and without, are not as the Bible suggests, 5,200, but may perhaps amount to 600,000?

. . . What have you to say about the countless millions who have *lived in the past?*

Outside the church no salvation: Can you keep on saying this when you look realistically at the *future,* and consider the statistics that show that the non-Christian nations of Asia and Africa are going by far to outstrip numerically the Christian nations of the West? . . . What have you to say about the innumerable millions and billions who are going to live in the future outside the Catholic church and altogether outside Christianity?[76]

This statement of Dr. Küng, which so vividly portrays how weak Christianity's efforts at conversion have been, despite a militant vocabulary, raises the question of conversion and makes it easy to write off the urgency to bring the world to a conscious awareness and acceptance of the claims of Jesus Christ, and to baptize these converts into the church.

This line of reasoning, however, is based on circumstantial evidence. The embarrassment a Christian might feel about either the techniques of missionary work in the past or the failure of church growth in the present is not determinative as to whether the mission of the church is to convert the world. Only theology and an investigation of the Biblical revelation can determine this. When we wanted to attack Kraemer's Biblical realism, we did not stand in some discipline other than theology in order to do so. Rather we considered the same ground and loyalty as Kraemer used, only working to a different conclusion. Similarly, in the matter of conversion, the directive for or against it must come from within.

However, here in the citadel of theology, the directive is not clear. Usually, theological exclusiveness has gone hand in hand with the mission to convert. This is understandable since with any form of exclusivism the line is drawn clearly between what is acceptable and what is not. As we said earlier, the great bulk of mission theology that has directed the modern expansion of Christianity has been dominated by theological exclusivism.[77] Contrariwise, it is the usual rule for theologians who hold an open view of Jesus Christ to be against conversion in the sense of proselytizing. Here are a few random statements:

E. Troeltsch: In relation to the great world religions we need to recognize that they are expressions of the religious consciousness corresponding to certain definite types of culture, and that it is their duty to increase in depth and purity by means of their own interior impulses, a task in which the contact with Christianity may prove helpful, to them as to us, in such processes of development from within. . . . *There can be no conversion or transformation of one into the other,* but only a measure of agreement and of mutual understanding.[78]

P. Tillich: In relation to Hinduism, Buddhism, and Taoism, we should continue the dialogue which has already started. . . . *Not conversion, but dialogue.* It would be a tremendous step forward if Christianity were to accept this! [79]

W. E. Hocking: If it were true . . . that without the doctrine of the *Only Way,* missions would lose their sufficient motive, I should accept that result. We cannot take it as a fixed premise that missions must go on.[80]

John Macquarrie, in his article "Christianity and Other Faiths," takes a similar stand when he writes:

In our time, this counter current [the attack on natural theology at the time of the Reformation] has become very important in the neo-Reformation theology associated with Karl Barth and others. However, the great and deserved influence of this school should not blind us to the fact that their claim that the knowledge of God is to be found exclusively in the Christian revelation is really a deviation (a most unfortunate one) from the Catholic or universal teaching of the greater part of the church throughout the greater part of its history.[81]

Macquarrie goes on to deny the possibility of any normative revelation, along with any imperialistic claims to "win the world." He even rejects Tillich's division of revelation into preparatory and final. The consequence, of course, is a denial of the need for the conversion of non-Christian peoples. The true purpose of missions, he says, is to spread love and truth, not to increase membership.

In the light of these quotations, it would seem that the directive from theology to the mission of the church is twofold: If theological exclusivism is embraced, then preach for conversion. If, on the other hand, theological inclusivism is taken, then give up the desire to convert people to a conscious awareness of Jesus Christ as Lord and Savior, and do not baptize such converts into the institutional church as an indication of this decision. However, it is our conviction that theological openness need not be tied to a counsel against conversion. Contrary to Tillich and others, we would like to maintain that however the Christian revelation be deepened, there must always be heard in Christian preaching the call to a decision to believe in the historic Christ. Without this, it would have to be admitted that the New Testament refrain, "Repent and be baptized," belonged to a rugged era that is no longer an example for today. This conclusion we will not draw. However, having said this, we will need to make a few qualifications.

First, since conversion is a transaction between God and man, and not primarily one between a person and a church organization, there is always the possibility of such a transaction's having occurred in any time and place *without* the knowledge or presence of an institutional representative of the Christian faith. Perhaps the poor way the institutional church has conducted its affairs or expressed its theology has prevented a formal stepping forth of many who have yet, in their inward soul, made a decision for God. That this could happen, the Christian theologian would still base on the activity of God in Christ. It is a silent effect of the incarnation and atonement. Beyond this general statement it is not wise to speculate.

There is a very suggestive treatment of the Prologue of John's Gospel that relates to this speculation. F. N. Davey deals with the statement in John 1:9 which refers to the logos: "The true light that enlightens every man was coming into the world." [82] He asks whether this reference to the "true light" should be interpreted in a Hellenistic fashion, referring to a general illumination of the minds of all men by the divine reason that was subsequently deepened by the complete manifestation in the incarnation. Along with C. K. Barrett, Davey rejects this interpretation. "To enlighten," he says, can mean "to illuminate inwardly," but it also has a less gentle use of "bringing to light" and "exposing to judgment," with a consequent decision being called for. This use seems more consistent with John's Gospel, as for instance, the use of "light" in John 3: 16–21. The conclusion of this, which, by the way, Davey does not draw and rather denies, is that wherever the logos has operated, there has been an exposure, a judgment, and a point of decision. We have no way of going beyond this to say what the decision was to, or how the light was conceptualized, or what activity followed the exposure. There are in the Old Testament hints of this revelation, in men like Melchizedek, Jethro, Balaam, Cyrus, and others, who stood outside the covenant and yet were affected by the "light." And, Karl Rahner seems to express it well when he says: "The church is the historical, visible vanguard—the historically and socially constituted expression of that which the Christian knows to exist as a hidden reality even outside the visibility of the church." [83] What is being defended is not speculation on the manner and outcome of conversion outside the church, but the firm statement of the possibility of its taking place times without number.

Secondly, there may be many cases where there is a conscious conversion to the Lordship of Jesus Christ without a formal acceptance of the Sacrament of Baptism or without an entrance into the Christian fellowship. As this was suggested earlier, we will not elaborate here. Suffice it to say that some Christian leaders, particularly in the younger churches, seem to be encouraging this open approach. Kaj Baago is one of these. He writes:

The missionary task of today cannot be to draw men out of their religion into another religion, but rather to go inside Hinduism and Buddhism, accepting these religions as one's own, in so far as they do not conflict with Christ, and regarding them as the presupposition, the background and framework of the Christian Gospel in Asia. Such a mission will not lead to the progress of Christianity or the organized church, but it might lead to the creation of Hindu Christianity or Buddhist Christianity.[84]

This position has great dangers if it is accepted as a general practice. That some are converted to Christ without acknowledging their conversion (or being acknowledged) through the Sacraments is one thing. That it should be a standard practice is quite another. The two who were chosen to criticize Baago's argument were quick to point this out—Ian Douglas, who heads the study center at Andhra Pradesh, and John B. Carman, who heads the Center for the Study of World Religions at Harvard. They said:

No known Christian will find it possible to disassociate himself from the Christian church and find acceptance in another religion, while still holding to Christian presuppositions. It is another question entirely what the Holy Spirit might do in the experience of those who really belong within these religions and are drawn to Jesus Christ.[85]

and again,

We have no new prophetic authority from God to accept this Gospel of Christ's redemption of the world, but to reject the human community through which the message of that redemption in word and deed, is conveyed to and somehow embodied in the world.[86]

This criticism of Baago seems valid. We might add a further criticism that if, with Baago, we encourage Hindu (or Buddhist) Christianity, the nerve of the Christian mission might be frayed to the breaking point. However, it does seem important to provide for the exceptional few to live as Christians within any of the world religions without being members of the organized church.

For Christian theologians to provide for this, i.e., Christians outside the visible community, leads to some interesting problems concerning the Sacraments and the church. Are the Sacraments, for instance, inexorably tied to conversion or only normally so? Or can the Sacraments be spiritualized much as the Roman Catholics do when they speak of the baptism of intention? And can the doctrine of the invisible church be revived so as to relate to such a contemporary problem as a confessing Christian who is also a confessing Hindu, Buddhist, Taoist, etc.? These are just a couple of questions that show that this thesis is in no sense complete without a much fuller treatment of Christian theology.

Thirdly, however Biblical theologians describe conversion and relate it to the convenant or to the Kingdom, conversion, in the laymen's meaning of the term, should be a guaranteed privilege of all groups and not just of the Christian church. Here the word is used, not as conversion to God, but rather as conversion to the truth as anyone happens to see it, together with the freedom to join that group which in his estimation expresses the truth the best. This has been a hotly debated issue in India. Recently, *Harijan,* a magazine carrying out the Gandhian tradition, carried an article in which it stated: "India when it stands for *no* evangelical work, stands on this basic principle of our religious and spiritual freedom." The argument was that conversion implied that one religion was right and the other wrong, and therefore was an intolerant attitude, which denied the Hindu genius.[87] Dr. Katju, the Home Minister, touched off more antimission debate on April 15, 1953, when he said: "If they [the missionaries] come here for evangelical work, the sooner they stop it the better." The attitude of Gandhi and the famous Niyogi Report against proselytism are well known.[88] How-

ever, the Indian Constitution, Article 25, continues to give
the freedom to any religion to profess, practice, and *propagate*. Nehru, himself, before he died, stated that he would
fight to the last ditch for the rights of minorities, and he repeatedly protested attacks upon Christianity. This is commendable, particularly when, at the time of his death, there
were some four thousand Christian missionaries in India.

Conversion, then, as the freedom of a religion to propagate
and of people to choose their religion, is an inherent human
right that should be protected in every national constitution.
Even Hocking—no particular friend of missions in the usual
sense—said, "I am prepared to fight for the rights of bigots
to do the mission work they feel impelled to do." [89]

Fourthly, "conversion," when applied to the change associated with the acceptance of Jesus Christ and entrance into
the church, must be devoid of the individualistic and senti-
mental connotations of Protestant piety. Usually the term
calls to mind an evangelical crusade or a preaching mission
in which the religious content is presented in an emotional
way. The listener is asked to make a decision to receive
the religious truths and realities that are set before him.
However, there are practical dangers in exaggerating these
common marks of evangelism. Most important is the fact
that spiritual ghettoism can be fostered on the mission field,
which men like D. T. Niles have protested. If conversion is
some warm, individualistic happening in the depths of one's
personality, it is easy to separate the spiritual from the secular, and to welcome the community that fostered the conversion experience at the expense of the world outside. When
that happens, an ingroup is formed that often feels little
concern for social justice and action. This was one of the
lesser fruits of the Pietist tradition of the late seventeenth
century. This danger is compounded when the conversion
experience is felt to be a dramatic event that is the criterion
for the experience of all other Christians. Is is no wonder
that with this background in American Protestantism, theo-

logical liberalism, among clergy and laity alike, has invari-
ably looked askance at the language of conversion.

However, despite these historically conditioned expressions, the call to conversion belongs to the central stuff of
the gospel, and that is why there was such a renewed study
of the term in the WCC in 1967. Some conclusions of this
study have wide acceptance and counteract the excesses that
have so discolored the word. One is that conversion in the
Bible is dependent entirely on God's initiative, and therefore
is not primarily a subject of group dynamics or missionary
techniques. It is God who answers the Hindu prayer: "From
the Unreal lead me to the real; from darkness to Light, from
death to immortality," and who answers it when and how
he chooses. Secondly, conversion is not an event of the past
that involves the acceptance of a precise number of doctrines.
Rather it is a dynamic movement. To return to the givenness
of the covenant means to become open to the future, to move
on with God toward his goals. Thirdly, conversion is in the
last analysis a secular act, in the sense that it does not involve
an affirmation of metaphysical beliefs, but concrete obedience
here and now. When the prophets insist that Israel is expected to have "steadfast love and not sacrifice, the knowledge of God, rather than burnt offerings" (Hos. 6:6), they
indicate an indissoluble relation between conversion and
social action.

In conclusion, we believe that conversion is a goal that is
consistent with theological openness. The desire to see conversion happen throughout the world must be as fervent in
a logos theologian as in the most ardent exclusivist. A casual
reading of the New Testament, particularly the book of The
Acts, strengthens this desire. So does a consideration of two
rather commonsense observations. The first is this. Whenever any person finds something vital, which he believes to
be indubitably true, he has an irresistible desire to share this
truth with others. This desire is present whether the truth
happens to be about God or not, although the more vital the

truth, the more fervent is the passion to share it. Furthermore, truth that is shared always calls forth some response
from the listener or conversant. Hocking is right when he
says of *reconception,* "The process does tend to a decision,
not through the conflict of faiths, or a campaign for world
dominance, but through the unforced persuasiveness of relative success in this effort to become a better vehicle of the
truth." [90] Therefore, a use of the word "conversion" in some
sense cannot be avoided. A presentation of the unbound
Christ calls for as much decision as a presentation of the
Christ of Biblical realism. In this regard, it is interesting that
Clement of Alexandria, who is the nemesis of Barthians, ap-
pealed strongly in his writings for conversion from unbelief,
while at the same time maintaining a continuity with the
philosophy and even the mystery religions of his time.[91]

This leads to a second observation. That which you conceive of as true, you hope will appeal to the widest number
of people. The prophets looked for the day when the knowledge of God would cover the earth as the waters cover the
sea. (Isa. 11:9.) This means that in all the reworking of
theological statement and in the coming dialogue, there is
always the Christian dream that Jesus Christ might com-
mand the *conscious* loyalty of all men, who will interpret
their own heritage and scripture from the light which comes
from the logos *en sarx* as well as the logos *en archē.* The
word "conversion" itself points to the fact of visible adher-
ence to the Christian faith. However, this does not mean that
the door is open for all kinds of offensive militant language
to return, nor for Western imperialism to be coupled with
the missionary motive. Certainly, as we have indicated, the
actual statistics of Christianity's evangelistic thrust are
enough to keep the Christian of the mid-twentieth century
humbled. But, for all this, the dream of a universal acceptance of the Christ persists and challenges Christian believers
of whatever theological persuasion.

To balance the incipient aggression in this dream along

with the needful humility produced by the Christian message itself, there should develop what might be called "a Gamalian approach" to missions. Gamaliel was the rabbi in the New Testament who was faced by Peter's not too gracious intolerance and said, "If this counsel or this work be of men, it will come to nought: But if it be of God, ye cannot overthrow it" (Act 5:38–39). His attitude, so expressed, might be a good one for the Christian missionary today. Gamaliel had his convictions concerning Judaism, and saw Christianity as a conflicting claim to truth. He no doubt favored the spread of Judaism as he then understood it, and the elimination of Christianity. However, he saw a way around the impasse caused by his reading of life and the contrary view of Simon Peter. This was to allow the final judge to be God himself rather than the Sanhedrin. He recognized that in the movement of men's convictions, the ultimate criterion is not numbers or doctrines, or "success," but the deep mystery that is indicated by the name of God.

Notes

INTRODUCTION

1. For a good, brief summary of the times in Christian history when the evangelical point of view controlled the Christian outlook, see Ernst Benz, "The Theological Meaning of the History of Religion," *Journal of Religion*, Vol. 41 (January, 1961), pp. 4–10.

2. Hendrik Kraemer, *The Christian Message in a Non-Christian World* (published for the International Missionary Council by Harper & Brothers, 1938), p. 106. Here Kraemer mentions the fear that mission motivation will deteriorate without his type of theology.

3. Kenneth Cragg, "Encounter with Non-Christian Faiths," *Union Seminary Quarterly Review*, Vol. 19, No. 4 (May, 1964), p. 305.

4. Julius Richter, "Missionary Apologetic: Its Problems and Its Methods," *International Review of Missions*, Vol. 2, pp. 520–541. It should be kept in mind that the "Science of Missions" was a new field. Richter states that it was Professor Warnecke, in 1890, who was the first to divide mission study into three fields that were later accepted by all Europeans: Mission History, Mission Theology, and Mission Apologetic.

5. *Ibid.*, pp. 540–541.

6. Wilfred C. Smith, "Comparative Religions: Whither and Why?" quoted in Mircea Eliade and Joseph M. Kitagawa (eds.), *The History of Religions: Essays in Methodology* (The University of Chicago Press, 1959), p. 31.

7. William Temple, quoted in Joseph M. Kitagawa, "Theology and the Science of Religion," *Anglican Theological Review*, Vol. 39 (1957), p. 34.

8. The terms "comparative religion," "history of religions," *"Religionswissenschaft,"* "science of religion," have operated without exact meaning and often with only an implied methodology. The terms are used interchangeably here. See Kitagawa, *loc. cit.,* p. 35.

9. Only a paragraph is given to methodology. For a fuller account, see the article in *Encyclopædia Britannica* entitled "Phenomenology," written by Husserl. Also, see Gerardus Van der Leeuw's *Religion in Essence and Manifestation* (London: George Allen & Unwin, Ltd., 1933), pp. 671–697.

10. This is based on a list in Van der Leeuw, *op. cit.,* Sec. 107, 2. For a similar list, see Herbert Spiegelberg, *The Phenomenological Movement* (The Hague: N. V. Martinus Nijhoff, 1965), Vol. 2, pp. 656 ff.

Chapter I. A CRITICAL APPROACH TO KRAEMER'S DOCTRINE OF REVELATION

1. Layman's Foreign Missions Inquiry, Commission of Appraisal, William E. Hocking, Chairman, *Re-Thinking Missions: A Layman's Inquiry After One Hundred Years* (Harper & Brothers, 1932).

2. *Ibid.,* p. 19.

3. *The Christian Message in a Non-Christian World* was written by Kraemer "at the request of the International Missionary Council in order to serve as material for the World Missionary Conference in 1938" (Preface, p. v). The conference, held at Madras, India, is herein referred to as the "Tambaram Conference," its common designation.

4. Hendrik Kraemer, "Continuity or Discontinuity," in *The Authority of the Faith,* Vol. I of The Tambaram Madras Series (published for the International Missionary Council by Oxford University Press, London, 1939). In this essay, Clement is used as the foil for Barth, with the latter receiving the favorable treatment. In the later book, *Religion and the Christian Faith* (London: Lutterworth Press, 1956), Kraemer gives a more sympathetic appreciation of Clement and other logos theologians (see Ch. 7, pp. 147–159).

5. See the excellent essay on "Revelation" by Barth in John

Baillie and Hugh Martin (eds.), *Revelation* (The Macmillan Company, 1937), pp. 41–83.

6. John Baillie, *The Idea of Revelation in Recent Thought* (Columbia University Press, 1956), pp. 19 ff.

7. Kraemer, *Religion and the Christian Faith,* pp. 439 ff.

8. Kraemer, *The Christian Message in a Non-Christian World,* pp. 69–85.

9. *Ibid.,* p. 83 (italics his).

10. See Kraemer, *Religion and the Christian Faith,* pp. 231–233, for a terse statement as to how the two books of Kraemer differ. He complains that he had said the dialectical "yes/no" in the first book, but people heard only the "no."

11. Karl Barth, *Church Dogmatics,* Vol. I, Part 2, ed. by G. W. Bromiley and T. F. Torrance (Charles Scribner's Sons, 1956), § 17, pp. 280–362.

12. Kraemer, *The Christian Message in a Non-Christian World,* p. 108.

13. *Ibid.*

14. Kraemer assumes that this distinction is easily maintained, without entering into the very critical problem of whether the church conditions the revelation or whether the revelation can be thought of apart from the historical church.

15. Kraemer, "Continuity or Discontinuity," *loc. cit.,* pp. 120–121.

16. *Ibid.,* p. 113.

17. *Ibid.*

18. *Ibid.,* p. 123 (italics mine). There is always the feeling that Kraemer is able to understand the "real meaning" of Bible verses.

19. Kraemer divides the Biblical support for Biblical realism into three categories: (*a*) Direct support (Rom. 1:19–32; Rom. 2:1–16; Rom. 3:29, 30; Acts 14:15–17; 17:16–37). (*b*) Indirect support (doctrines such as the Creation and the Fall, the covenant of Noah, Wisdom literature, the logos concept, etc.). (*c*) Concepts such as "people," "community," "Gentiles," etc.

20. A very useful book by Gerald Cooke, *As Christians Face Rival Religions* (Association Press, 1962), devotes two chapters to what he calls "simplicism," namely, the areas in different religions that look the same and yet are quite different underneath.

However, contrary to Kraemer's viewpoint, Cooke shows many other areas that look different on the surface but really are quite similar.

21. W. A. Visser 't Hooft, *No Other Name* (The Westminster Press, 1963).

22. Lesslie Newbigen, *Trinitarian Faith and Today's Mission* (John Knox Press, 1964).

23. Edmund Perry, *The Gospel in Dispute: The Relation of Christian Faith to Other Missionary Religions* (Doubleday & Company, Inc., 1958).

24. Heinrich Frick, *The Gospel, Christianity and Other Religions* (London: Oxford University Press, 1938).

25. William E. Hocking, *Living Religions and a World Faith* (The Macmillan Company, 1940), p. 169.

26. Karl Barth, *Church Dogmatics*, G. T. Thompson, trans., Vol. I, Part 1 (Charles Scribner's Sons, 1936), § 4, pp. 98–141.

27. Kraemer, *The Christian Message in a Non-Christian World*, p. 73.

28. H. H. Farmer, "The Authority of the Faith," in *The Authority of the Faith*, p. 152.

29. Stephen Neill, *Creative Tension* (London: Edinburgh House Press, 1959), pp. 24 ff.

30. Kraemer, "Continuity or Discontinuity," *loc. cit.*, p. 4.

31. Karl Barth, "Revelation," in Baillie and Martin (eds.), *op. cit.*, p. 62.

32. This view of Barth's is not far from Tillich's discussion of primary and secondary symbols. See Paul Tillich, *Systematic Theology*, 3 vols. (The University of Chicago Press, 1951, 1957, 1963), Vol. I, pp. 126 ff.

33. Cooke, *op. cit.*, pp. 149–150.

34. Kraemer, *The Christian Message in a Non-Christian World*, p. 108.

35. A. G. Hogg, "The Christian Attitude to Non-Christian Faith," in *The Authority of the Faith*, pp. 94–114.

36. *Ibid.*, p. 98.

37. Kraemer, *The Christian Message in a Non-Christian World*, p. 61.

38. *Ibid.*, p. 208, italics his.

39. Perry, *op. cit.*, p. 220.

40. Kraemer, "Continuity or Discontinuity," *loc. cit.*, p. 7.

Chapter II. A CONSTRUCTIVE APPROACH
TO THE DOCTRINE OF REVELATION

1. Canon Lilley, *Religion and Revelation* (London: S.P.C.K., 1932). Cf. p. 119: "Now Theology has . . . broken with the old tradition. But, it has done so incidentally, and almost unconsciously."

2. Baillie and Martin (eds.), *op. cit.*, p. x.

3. William Temple, *Nature, Man and God* (The Macmillan Company, 1951).

4. *Ibid.*, p. 27.

5. *Ibid.*, p. 17.

6. *Ibid.*, p. 16.

7. *Ibid.*, p. 306.

8. The modernity of the new distinction of "special" and "general" revelation has sometimes been called into question. John Baillie agrees that the full development of the usage is modern, though it was hinted at by older writers. See Baillie and Martin (eds.), *op. cit.*, p. xviii.

9. Gerhard Kittel and Gerhard Friedrich (eds.), *Theological Dictionary of the New Testament*, 4 vols. (Wm. B. Eerdmans Publishing Company, 1964, 1965, 1966, 1967).

10. Baillie, *op. cit.*, pp. 32 f.

11. Tillich, *Systematic Theology,* Vol. I, p. 109.

12. Baillie, *op. cit.*, p. 59.

13. S. Bulgakoff, "Revelation," in Baillie and Martin (eds.), *op. cit.*, pp. 147 f.

14. John Baillie, quoted in E. L. Wenger, "The Problem of Truth in Religion," in E. A. Payne, *Studies in History and Religion* (London: Lutterworth Press, 1942), p. 164.

15. We are using the words "fallible" and "infallible" here even though they have more relevance to revelation as propositional truth rather than as communion. To speak of "infallible relationships" between human beings is almost an absurd use of terms.

16. Thomas Aquinas, *Summa Theologica*, Part I, Q. lxviii, Art. i; quoted in Temple, *Nature, Man and God,* p. 310.

17. Karl Barth, *Church Dogmatics,* Vol. I, Part 1, pp. 98–141.

18. Wenger, *loc. cit.,* p. 164.

19. Austin Farrer, *The Glass of Vision* (London: Novello & Company, Ltd., 1948). We shall be concerned with Lecture III, pp. 35–56.

20. *Ibid.,* p. 35.

21. *Ibid.*

22. *Ibid.,* p 37.

23. *Ibid.,* p. 42.

24. *Ibid.,* pp. 42 f.

25. Wenger, *loc. cit.,* pp. 169 ff.

26. Alan Richardson, *Christian Apologetics* (Harper & Brothers, 1947), p. 130.

27. Walter Horton, "Revelation," in Baillie and Martin (eds.), *op. cit.,* pp. 263–264.

28. H. Richard Niebuhr, *The Meaning of Revelation* (The Macmillan Company, 1962), p. 42.

29. *Ibid.,* Preface, p. x. "I have tried to combine their main interests, for it appears to me that the critical thought of the former and the constructive work of the latter belong together."

30. *Ibid.,* p. 18.

31. *Ibid.,* p. 20.

32. Nathan Söderblom, *The Nature of Revelation,* tr. from the 1st German ed. of 1903 (Oxford University Press, Inc., 1933), p. 8.

33. *Ibid.,* pp. 29 f., 43 f. Söderblom divided all world religions into cultural religions, where the mysticism of infinity was characteristic, and prophetic religions, where the mysticism of personality was characteristic.

34. *Ibid.,* p. 43 (italics mine).

35. Söderblom, quoted in E. Ehnmark, "General Revelation According to Nathan Söderblom," *Journal of Religion,* Vol. 35 (1955), p. 224.

36. Robert L. Slater, *World Religions and World Community* (Columbia University Press, 1963).

37. *Ibid.,* p. 164.

38. Niebuhr, *op. cit.,* p. 22.

Chapter III. REVELATION AND LOGOS

1. Justin Martyr, *Apologia* I. xlvi, quoted in H. Bettenson, *The Early Christian Fathers* (London: Oxford University Press, 1956), p. 83.

2. William Temple, *Readings in the Gospel of John* (London: The Macmillan Company, 1940), p. 10.

3. See the argument in A. C. Bouquet, *The Christian Faith and Non-Christian Religions* (London: James Nisbet & Co., Ltd., 1958), p. 146; and in his "Revelation and the Divine Logos," in Gerald Anderson (ed.), *The Theology of the Christian Mission* (McGraw-Hill Book Company, Inc., 1961), pp. 183–184.

4. E. R. Goodenough says that the personal statements are due to the way that the logos was the agent of deliverance for Philo. Philo writes: "They who have real knowledge of the one Creator and Father of all things are rightly addressed as the sons of the one God. And even if we are not yet fit to be called sons of God, still we may deserve to be called the children of His eternal image, of His most sacred logos" (*Conf. ling.* 28). Yet, says Goodenough, if Philo were asked if the logos were personal, he would no doubt go back to his pure metaphysical monotheism. See E. R. Goodenough, *An Introduction to Philo Judeus* (Yale University Press, 1940), p. 102.

5. Eric L. Titus, *The Message of the Fourth Gospel* (Abingdon Press, 1947), p. 45.

6. A. C. Bouquet, *op. cit.*, p. 148.

7. Cf. W. R. Inge, "Logos," *Encyclopedia of Religion and Ethics*, ed. by James Hastings, Vol. 8, p. 136. Inge comments that the creative function of the logos is not stressed in the Prologue because the Father is not a transcendent being who finds it impossible to act directly on the world.

8. Kraemer, *Religion and the Christian Faith*, p. 280.

9. James Barr, *The Semantics of Biblical Language* (London: Oxford University Press, 1961). See especially the chapter "Some Principles of Kittel's Theological Dictionary," pp. 206–263.

10. Quoted by Barr, *op. cit.*, p. 221, from Kittel's *Theological Dictionary of the New Testament*, Vol. IV, p. 788.

11. Raymond Panikkar, *The Unknown Christ of Hinduism* (London: Darton, Longman and Todd, Ltd., 1965), p. 51.

12. Bouquet, "Revelation and the Divine Logos," *loc. cit.*, pp. 193 ff.

13. E. L. Allen, *Christianity Among the Religions* (Beacon Press, 1960), p. 124. For a similar point of view, see G. Parrinder, *Comparative Religion* (London: George Allen & Unwin, Ltd., 1962), pp. 47–55.

14. Paul Lehmann, "The Logos in a World Come of Age," *Theology Today*, Vol. 21, No. 3 (Oct., 1964), pp. 274–286.

15. Lehmann, *loc. cit.*, p. 282. Cf. Tillich, *Systematic Theology*, Vol. II, pp. 138–139.

16. J. A. Cuttat, *The Encounter of Religions: A Dialogue Between the West and the Orient, with an Essay on the Prayer of Jesus* (Desclee Co., Inc., 1957).

17. *Ibid.*, p. 30.

18. *Ibid.*, p. 73, italics mine.

19. Of the writings that deal specifically with this problem, see Ernst Benz, "On Understanding Non-Christian Religions," in Eliade and Kitagawa, *op. cit.*, pp. 115–132; his "The Theological Meaning of the History of Religions," *loc. cit.;* and his "Ideas for a Theology of the History of Religion," in Gerald Anderson (ed.), *The Theology of the Christian Mission*, pp. 135–147.

20. Paul D. Devanandan, "The Resurgence of Non-Christian Religions," in Gerald Anderson (ed.), *The Theology of the Christian Mission*, pp. 151–152.

21. See Albert van den Heuvel, "Secularization as Freedom and Yoke," in *Study Encounter*, Vol. 1, No. 2 (1965), published by the World Council of Churches, pp. 55–63.

22. Most contemporary theologians distinguish between secularization and secularism. The former is the process by which man and society are liberated from the control of metaphysics and theology. The latter is an ideology that denies the existence of metaphysical realities and becomes a historical materialism.

23. L. Kleever, "Mapping Radical Theologies," *Religion in Life*, Vol. 36 (1967), pp. 8–28.

24. Arend Van Leeuwen, *Christianity in World History* (Charles Scribner's Sons, 1964).

25. *Ibid.*, pp. 264 f., a quote from Carl F. von Weizsäcker, *Zum Weltbild der Physik* (Stuttgart, 6th ed., 1954).

26. K. M. Panikkar, quoted in Van Leeuwen, *op. cit.*, p. 269.

27. Kaj Baago sees the effect of secularization quite differently from Van Leeuwen. He writes: "But although secularization is world wide, it is ridiculous to think the days of the Eastern Religions are over. . . . A Hindu secularization is not the same as a Christian secularization." "The Post-Colonial Crisis of Missions," *International Review of Missions,* Vol. 56 (1967), p. 102.

28. Floyd Ross, "The Christian Mission in Larger Dimension," in Gerald Anderson (ed.), *The Theology of the Christian Mission,* p. 219.

29. For an excellent discussion of exclusivist Bible verses, see E. C. Dewick, *The Christian Attitude to Other Religions* (London: Cambridge University Press, 1953), pp. 92–95.

30. Robert E. Speer, in *Reports,* Vol. I, pp. 428 ff., quoted in Dewick, *op. cit.,* p. 143.

31. Robert E. Speer, in *The Christian Life and Message in Relation to Non-Christian Systems of Thought and Life,* Vol. I of *The Jerusalem Meeting of the International Missionary Council, March 24–April 8, 1928,* 8 vols. (London: Oxford University Press, 1928), p. 143.

32. Report of the Archbishop's Commission, *Doctrine in the Church of England* (London: S.P.C.K., 1938), p. 76.

33. Dewick, *op. cit.,* p. 114.

34. Kraemer, *The Christian Message in a Non-Christian World,* p. 6.

35. See Bouquet's essay in Gerald Anderson (ed.), *The Theology of the Christian Mission,* p. 198. Also see the Epilogue of Bouquet's book *The Christian Faith and Non-Christian Religions,* p. 424.

36. D. T. Niles, *Upon the Earth* (McGraw-Hill Book Company, Inc., 1962), p. 40.

37. Hocking, *op. cit.,* p. 187.

38. Quoted in N. Macnichol, *Is Christianity Unique?* (London: SCM Press, Ltd., 1936), p. 168.

39. Karl Barth, *The Humanity of God* (John Knox Press, 1960), p. 59.

Chapter IV. THE EXPERIENCE OF THE LOGOS

1. Rudolf Otto deals with Bhakti in *India's Religion of Grace and Christianity* tr. by Frank Hugh Foster (SCM Press, Ltd.,

1930); he treats Vedanta in *Mysticism East and West* (Meridian Books, Inc., 1957).

2. Tillich, *Systematic Theology*, Vol. I, p. 79.

3. Tillich, *Biblical Religion and the Search for Ultimate Reality* (The University of Chicago Press, 1951), p. 85.

4. D. M. Brown, *Ultimate Concern: Tillich in Dialogue* (Harper & Row, Publishers, Inc., 1965), p. 46.

5. Claude Welch records a conversation with Tillich, in which the latter observed that while he was strongly influenced by Luther, he was one of the few German theologians who had not written on Luther.

6. Tillich, *Biblical Religion and the Search for Ultimate Reality*, p. 85.

7. Rudolf Otto, *The Idea of the Holy* (Oxford University Press, Inc., 1950), Ch. 12. Though *Das Heilige* went through twenty-five publications between 1917 and 1936, scarcely any full commentaries have appeared on his work. A notable exception is Robert F. Davidson's *Rudolf Otto's Interpretation of Religion* (Princeton University Press, 1947).

8. Charles A. Bennett, "Religion and the Idea of the Holy," *Journal of Philosophy*, Vol. 23 (August, 1926), p. 460.

9. John M. Moore, *Theories of Religious Experience* (Round Table Press, 1938), p. 91.

10. Davidson, *op. cit.*, p. 97, quoting H. Hoffding, *The Philosophy of Religion* (The Macmillan Company, 1914).

11. Davidson, *op. cit.*, p. 54.

12. Otto, *The Idea of the Holy*, Ch. 18, "The Manifestations of the 'Holy' and Faculty of 'Divination,' " pp. 147 ff.

13. *Ibid.*, p. 46.

14. Cf. a penetrating criticism in John Macquarrie, *Twentieth-Century Religious Thought* (Harper & Row, Publishers, Inc., 1963), pp. 216, 224.

15. See footnote 5 in Davidson, *op. cit.*, p. 52, in which he gives a long list of distinguished scholars who have accepted Otto's concept of numinous feeling and adopted it themselves.

16. Otto, *The Idea of the Holy*, p. 103.

17. *Ibid.*, p. 8.

18. *Ibid.*, p. 10. Gen. 18:27 is used as an illustration.

19. *Ibid.*, pp. 13–24.

20. *Ibid.*, p. 21.

21. *Ibid.*, p. 24.

22. *Ibid.*, Ch. 5, pp. 25 ff. See also Ch. 9 of the *Religious Essays* (London: Oxford University Press, 1931), where he gives added descriptions from religious history and theology.

23. *Ibid.*, p. 26.

24. *Ibid.*, p. 28. Otto often quotes Augustine as backing up his interpretation of the religious experience. In *Confessions* ii, 9, 1, for instance, Augustine very strikingly suggests this stiffening, benumbing element of the Wholly Other and its contrast to the rational aspect of the numen.

25. *Ibid.*, pp. 31 ff.

26. *Ibid.*, Foreword.

27. Peter Munz, *Problems of Religious Knowledge* (London: SCM Press, Ltd., 1959), pp. 118–119.

28. Otto, *The Idea of the Holy,* p. 94.

29. *Ibid.*, p. 178.

30. See Davidson, *op. cit.*, p. 73; also, J. Wach, *Types of Religious Experience, Christian and Non-Christian* (The University of Chicago Press, 1951), pp. 209 f., where he feels that neo-orthodoxy needs Otto's approach for completeness and to prevent a gross imbalance.

31. John W. Oman, *The Natural and the Supernatural* (London: Cambridge University Press, 1931), p. 58.

32. *Ibid.*, p. 72.

33. John W. Oman, quoted in Macquarrie, *op. cit.*, p. 217.

34. Herbert H. Farmer, *Revelation and Religion* (London: James Nisbet & Co., Ltd., 1954).

35. *Ibid.*, p. 44, quoted from Oman, *op. cit.*, p. 57.

36. Farmer, *op. cit.*, p. 66.

37. Carl Jung, quoted in Farmer, *op. cit.*, p. 67.

38. Otto, *The Idea of the Holy,* pp. 130–132, quoted in Farmer, *op. cit.*, pp. 68–69.

39. Farmer, *op. cit.*, p. 76.

40. *Ibid.*, pp. 78–79.

41 Kraemer, *Religion and the Christian Faith*, p. 220.

42. Macquarrie, *op. cit.*, p. 344.

Chapter V. THE LOGOS AND RADICAL CHRISTIANITY

1. Paul Tillich, *The Future of Religions*, ed. by Jerald D. Brauer (Harper & Row, Publishers, Inc., 1966), p. 83. This is the same criticism that John Macquarrie directs to van Buren in his article "How Can We Think of God," *Theology Today*, July, 1965.

2. J. H. Randall remarks about Tillich's ontology: "The difficulty arises not when I discover that as a philosopher I am a theologian, but when I find that to be a good philosopher and answer my questions, I must be a Christian theologian." Quoted from *The Theology of Paul Tillich*, ed. by C. W. Kegley and R. W. Bretall (The Macmillan Company, 1952), p. 141.

3. Paul Tillich, "The Two Types of Philosophy," *Union Seminary Quarterly Review*, Vol. I, No. 4 (May, 1946), pp. 13–14.

4. Paul Tillich, "How My Mind Has Changed," *The Christian Century*, Dec. 6, 1960, p. 1435.

5. Tillich, *Systematic Theology*, Vol. I, pp. 71 ff.

6. *Ibid.*, Vol. I, p. 28.

7. Tillich, "How My Mind Has Changed," *loc. cit.*, p. 1436.

8. Tillich, *Systematic Theology*, Vol. I, pp. 238–239. It should be noted that Tillich softens this statement in Vol. II (p. 9). "The question arises . . . as to whether there is a point at which a non-symbolic assertion about God must be made. There is such a point, namely the statement that everything we say about God is symbolic."

9. Paul Tillich, *Christianity and the Encounter of the World Religions* (Columbia University Press, 1963), p. 4.

10. *Ibid.*, Vol. I, p. 221.

11. *Ibid.*, Vol. I, p. 17.

12. *Ibid.*, Vol. I, pp. 133–136.

13. *Ibid.*, Vol. I, p. 134. See also Tillich, *The Future of Religions*, pp. 88 ff.

14. Tillich, *Christianity and the Encounter of the World Religions*, p. 32.

15. There is a certain ambiguity in Tillich in his use of the polar terms "concrete-universal" and "concrete-ultimate." He

seems to interchange "universal" and "ultimate" without stating the relationship between them.

16. Tillich, *Christianity and the Encounter of the World Religions,* p. 34; also see Augustine, *Librum de vera Religione,* Ch. 10.

17. *Ibid.,* p. 97.

18. *Ibid.,* p. 64.

19. Tillich, *Systematic Theology,* Vol. I, p. 219.

20. Nicolas Berdyaev, *The Meaning of History* (London: The Centenary Press, Geoffrey Bles, Ltd., 1936), p. 197.

21. Albert Schweitzer, *Christianity and the Religions of the World* (The Macmillan Company, 1923).

22. Albert Schweitzer, *Indian Thought and Its Development* (Henry Holt & Co., Inc., 1936).

23. S. Radhakrishnan, *Eastern Religions and Western Thought* (Oxford University Press, 1959), p. 68.

24. *Ibid.,* Sec. XI, pp. 105 ff.

25. Tillich, *Systematic Theology,* Vol. I, p. 151.

26. Tillich, *Christianity and the Encounter of the World Religions,* pp. 32 f.

27. Tillich, "How My Mind Has Changed," *loc. cit.,* p. 1435.

28. Dietrich Bonhoeffer, *Christ the Center,* tr. by John Bowden (Harper & Brothers, 1960), pp. 71–77.

29. Paul Tillich, in Brown, *Ultimate Concern: Tillich in Dialogue.*

Chapter VI. THEOLOGICAL OPENNESS AND THE MISSION OF THE CHURCH

1. See Paul D. Devanandan, "Hindu Missions to the West," *International Review of Missions* (hereafter abbreviated as *I.R.M.*), Vol. 48, No. 192, pp. 398–408; also, W. Holsten, "Buddhism in Germany," *I.R.M.,* Vol. 48, No. 192, pp. 409–421; and Wendell Thomas, *Hinduism Invades America* (Beacon Press, 1930).

2. Division of Studies, World Council of Churches, "The Word of God and the Living Faiths of Men," a mimeographed document for study and discussion, July, 1958, p. 1.

3. Johannes Blauw, *The Missionary Nature of the Church* (McGraw-Hill Book Company, Inc., 1962).

4. D. T. Niles is one of the ecumenical leaders of Ceylon, India.

5. Gerald Anderson (ed.), *The Theology of the Christian Mission*, p. 13. Kenneth S. Latourette gives an even higher percentage if only the U.S.A. is considered. He writes that in 1910, the large majority of missionaries from the U.S.A. came from societies represented at Edinburgh. Now half come from those not cooperating. He raises the question of whether this is due to the growth of younger churches and the decline of colonialism, or to a loss of meaning of the gospel. See Kenneth Scott Latourette, "Developments in the Younger Churches Since Edinburgh 1910," *Religion in Life*, Vol. 29 (Summer, 1960), p. 353.

6. For a good defense of this position, see H. Lindsell, "Fundamentals for a Philosophy of the Christian Mission," in Gerald Anderson (ed.), *The Theology of the Christian Mission*, pp. 239–250.

7. W. M. Buschman states the case too strongly when he says: "It is the tragic fact of missionary history that it has been left to representatives of fundamentalism, pietism and other distorted theological systems to interpret Christianity to other religions." Quoted from "Theology and the Non-Christian Religions," *Theology Today*, Vol. 16, No. 4 (Jan., 1960), p. 459. Yet this overstatement does show the strong exclusivist position that exists outside as well as inside the World Council of Churches.

8. See Hocking, *op. cit.*, Lecture II, "Some Characteristics of Oriental Religion," esp. Sec. B, "Relative Formlessness."

9. Bouquet, "Revelation and the Divine Logos," *loc. cit.*, p. 198.

10. Kaj Baago, "The Post-Colonial Crisis of Missions: A Reply," *I.R.M.*, Vol. 56, No. 221 (1967), p. 102.

11. J. C. Hoekendijk, *The Church Inside Out* (The Westminster Press, 1966).

12. Wilfrid C. Smith, *The Meaning and End of Religion* (The Macmillan Company, 1963).

13. Hoekendijk, *op. cit.*, p. 40 (italics mine).

14. The term "fourth man" and its characterization comes from Alfred Weber, *Kulturgeschichte als Kultursoziologie* (1950). See Hoekendijk's discussion, *op. cit.*, Ch. 3, pp. 47 ff.

15. Hoekendijk, *op. cit.*, p. 73.

16. The church-oriented positions, which, interestingly enough, are usually combined with exclusivist theology, are represented in R. K. Strachan, "The Call to Witness," *I.R.M.*, 1964, pp. 191–200; M. Barth, "What Is the Gospel?" *I.R.M.*, 1964, pp. 441–449; Donald McGavran, "Wrong Strategy, Real Crisis in Missions," *I.R.M.*, 1965, pp. 451–461. The more open approach to the world is seen in V. E. Haywood, "Call to Witness, but What Kind of Witness," *I.R.M.*, 1964, pp. 201–208; Kaj Baago, "The Post-Colonial Crisis of Missions," *I.R.M.*, 1966, pp. 322–332.

17. Wilhelm Andersen, "Further Toward a Theology of Mission," in Gerald Anderson (ed.), *The Theology of the Christian Mission*, pp. 300–312.

18. Smith, *The Meaning and End of Religion*, p. 201.

19. *Ibid.*, p. 32. See the long explanatory note and defense of this statement—footnote 61, pp. 217–218.

20. *Ibid.*, p. 61.

21. *Ibid.* Cf. Ch. 5, "Is the Concept Adequate?"

22. *Ibid.*, p. 137.

23. See the interesting letter on this subject, reprinted in Robert L. Slater's "The Prospects of Dialogue," *Theology*, Vol. LXIX, No. 550 (April, 1966), p. 2.

24. At a recent Anglican Congress in Toronto, the theme of the "listening church" was a very prominent one. See *1963 Anglican Congress: Report of Proceedings*, ed. by E. R. Fairweather (Toronto, 1963).

25. For the address and the information given below, see U Kyaw Than, "The Christian Mission in Asia Today," *I.R.M.*, Vol. 47 (1958), pp. 153–162.

26. *Ibid.*, p. 159.

27. This episode is recorded in Slater, *op. cit.*, pp. 5–6, who recorded it from Winston L. King, *Buddhism and Christianity: Some Bridges of Understanding* (The Westminster Press, 1962), pp. 34 ff.

28. Hocking first made this proposal in a pamphlet entitled "Evangelism."

29. A list of various study centers can be found in the *Occasional Bulletin* of the Missionary Research Library (3041 Broadway, N.Y. 10027), Vol. XII, No. 4 (April 25, 1961).

30. See particularly Kraemer, *Religion and the Christian Faith,* p. 391.

31. See the interesting defense of this thesis by D. T. Niles in his contribution to Gerald Anderson (ed.), *Sermons to Men of Other Faiths and Traditions* (Abingdon Press, 1966), pp. 75–91.

32. Cragg, "Encounter with Non-Christian Faiths," *loc. cit.,* p. 309.

33. The following quotations are from *The New Delhi Report,* The Third Assembly of the World Council of Churches, 1961 (Association Press, 1962).

34. The underlined part was later omitted and replaced by a quotation of John 1:9, that Christ is the "light that enlightens every man."

35. This section of the report was the most sharply debated of the entire report, several theologians asking if we had any authority to speak of the activity of God outside his revelation in Christ.

36. See G. Johnston, "The Christian Mission and Christ's Prevenience," in *Theology Today,* April, 1963, pp. 31–42, where the author fears the New Delhi report will cut down on missionary zeal.

37. Cf. Kraemer, *The Christian Message in a Non-Christian World,* pp. 200–211; *Religion and the Christian Faith,* Ch. 24, "Syncretism as a Problem for Religion"; and Kraemer's letter in Gerald Anderson (ed.), *The Theology of the Christian Mission,* pp. 179–183.

38. See especially Baago "The Post-Colonial Crisis of Missions: A Reply," *loc. cit.,* pp. 99–103.

39. *Ibid.,* p. 101.

40. *Ibid.*

41. *Ibid.,* p. 102.

42. Kraemer, *Religions and the Christian Faith,* p. 391.

43. *Ibid.,* p. 390.

44. Philip H. Ashby, in his *The History and Future of Religious Thought* (Prentice-Hall, Inc., 1963), pp. 154 f., calls attention to the need to study what happens when a religion leaves the primary culture of its origin and becomes implanted in a secondary culture. Such a study, he feels, would lead to greater understanding of the movement of religions today.

45. Cf. R. P. Beaver, "Why Ram Christianity Down Their Throats?" *World Encounter,* Vol. III, No. 2 (Dec., 1965), p. 12.

46. For a historical presentation of how this emphasis was reached, and also what it might mean for the future encounter of religions, see W. C. Smith's essay, "Comparative Religion, Whither and Why?" *loc. cit.,* pp. 31–58.

47. Slater, *op. cit.,* p. 150.

48. Reuel Howe, *The Miracle of Dialogue* (The Seabury Press, Inc., 1963).

49. *Ibid.,* p. 37.

50. *Ibid.,* p. 10.

51. *Ibid.,* p. 65.

52. *Ibid.,* pp. 65–66.

53. *Ibid.,* p. 105.

54. *Ibid.,* p. 40.

55. The thought of the latter part of this sentence Howe later develops under the heading of "correlative thinking," *ibid.,* p. 42.

56. *Ibid.,* p. 10.

57. *Ibid.,* p. 15.

58. Douglas V. Steere, "Mutual Irradiation," *Religion in Life,* Vol. 28 (1958–1959), pp. 395–405.

59. *Ibid.,* p. 400.

60. Wilfrid C. Smith, *Islam in Modern History* (Princeton University Press, 1957), p. 104, n. 11.

61. Charles Malik, quoted from an essay, "The Near East: The Search for Truth," in *Foreign Affairs,* 1952, p. 258, and quoted in Neill, *op. cit.,* p. 61.

62. Muhammad Kamel Hussein, "City of Wrong," printed in full in *Christianity, Some Non-Christian Appraisals,* ed. by David W. McKain (McGraw-Hill Book Company, 1964), pp. 257–277.

63. Kraemer, *World Cultures and World Religions* (The Westminster Press, 1961), p. 364, n. 1.

64. Huston Smith, "Between Syncretism and the Ghetto," *Theology Today,* Vol. XX, No. 1 (April, 1963), pp. 21–30.

65. Kenneth Cragg, "Man and Empire: God and Forgiveness," printed in Gerald Anderson (ed.), *Sermons to Men of Other Faiths and Traditions,* pp. 91–101.

66. Leroy Rouner reports that Baago's work will soon be published under the title *Hindu Christianity.* See Leroy Rouner, "Re-

thinking the Christian Mission to India Today," *Religion in Life,* Vol. 35, No. 4 (Autumn, 1966), p. 533.

67. Panikkar, *The Unknown Christ of Hinduism,* p. 39.

68. *Ibid.,* p. 17.

69. *Ibid.,* p. 54.

70. *Ibid.,* p. 113.

71. *Ibid.,* p. 136.

72. Cf. the U.S. Conference for the World Council of Churches held at Buck Hill Falls, Pa., April, 1967, where the theme was "Conversion." Also, cf. the Division of Studies magazine *Study Encounter* for 1965, Vol. 1, No. 2, which is devoted to "Secularization and Conversion."

73. See an able discussion of this question in A. G. Hogg's book, *The Christian Message to the Hindu* (London: SCM Press, Ltd., 1947), especially Ch. 3, "Come Join My Church," pp. 39–57.

74. From C. F. Pascoe, *Two Hundred Years of the S.P.C.K.* (London: 1901)—a quote of E. C. Weldon recorded also in Baago, "The Post-Colonial Crisis of Missions," *loc. cit.,* p. 323.

75. *Ibid.,* p. 76.

76. Hans Küng, "The World Religions and God's Plan of Salvation," *Indian Ecclesiastical Studies,* July–October, 1965, pp. 184 ff.

77. E. C. Dewick quotes missionaries who would not feel it is the obligation for converts to leave their old religious community and join a Christian church, but he admits these missionaries are exceptions. See Dewick, *op. cit.,* pp. 188 f.

78. E. Troeltsch, "The Place of Christianity Among the Religions," Ernst Troeltsch, *Christian Thought: Its History and Application* (Meridian Books, 1957), pp. 58–59 (italics mine).

79. Tillich, *Christianity and the Encounter of the World Religions,* p. 95 (italics mine).

80. Hocking, *op. cit.,* p. 174.

81. John Macquarrie, "Christianity and Other Faiths," *Union Seminary Quarterly Review,* Vol. 20, No. 1 (Nov., 1964), pp. 39–48.

82. F. N. Davey, "The Gospel According to St. John and the Christian Mission," in Gerald Anderson (ed.), *The Theology of the Christian Mission,* pp. 85–95.

83. Karl Rahner, quoted in Gabriel Moran, *Theology of Revelation* (Herder & Herder, Inc., 1966), p. 177.

84. Baago, "The Post-Colonial Crisis of Missions," *loc. cit.*, p. 332.

85. Ian H. Douglas and John B. Carman, "The Post-Colonial Crisis of Missions: Comments," *I.R.M.*, Vol. 55 (Oct., 1966), p. 486.

86. *Ibid.*, p. 487.

87. See C. Foreman, "Freedom of Conversion, The Issue in India," *I.R.M.*, Vol. 45 (1956), pp. 180–193.

88. It is often forgotten, as E. L. Cattell reports, that M. B. Niyogi, former Chief Justice of the Nagpur High Court, who produced the Niyogi Report, was himself among the 75,000 who, on Oct. 14, 1956, went through the ritual of being converted to Buddhism following the decision of Dr. Ambedkar. See E. L. Cattell, "The Christian Impact on India," *I.R.M.*, Vol. 51 (1962), pp. 153–162.

89. Hocking, *op. cit.*, p. 176.

90. *Ibid.*, p. 201.

91. Cf. W. E. Nogren, "Conversion as an Ecumenical Problem," paper read before the U.S. Conference for the World Council of Churches, Buck Hill Falls, Pa., April 20, 1967, p. 2 (mimeographed).

Index of Proper Names

215

Index of Subjects